ISBN 978-1-333-73705-4
PIBN 10541299

1 MONTH OF
FREE
READING

at

www.ForgottenBooks.com

By purchasing this book you are eligible for one month membership to ForgottenBooks.com, giving you unlimited access to our entire collection of over 700,000 titles via our web site and mobile apps.

To claim your free month visit:

www.forgottenbooks.com/free541299

English
Français
Deutsche
Italiano
Español
Português

www.forgottenbooks.com

Mythology Photography **Fiction**
Fishing Christianity **Art** Cooking
Essays Buddhism Freemasonry
Medicine **Biology** Music **Ancient
Egypt** Evolution Carpentry Physics
Dance Geology **Mathematics** Fitness
Shakespeare **Folklore** Yoga Marketing
Confidence Immortality Biographies
Poetry **Psychology** Witchcraft
Electronics Chemistry History **Law**
Accounting **Philosophy** Anthropology
Alchemy Drama Quantum Mechanics
Atheism Sexual Health **Ancient History**
Entrepreneurship Languages Sport
Paleontology Needlework Islam
Metaphysics Investment Archaeology
Parenting Statistics Criminology
Motivational

The History of the Russian Revolution to Brest-Litovsk

By L. TROTSKY

LONDON: GEORGE ALLEN & UNWIN LTD.
RUSKIN HOUSE   40 MUSEUM STREET, W.C. 1

First published in 1919

INTRODUCTION

THE present booklet was, for the most part, written in snatches, in circumstances but little favourable to concentrated work. It was at Brest-Litovsk, between the sittings of the Peace Conference, that the different chapters of this sketch, which has for its main purpose to acquaint the workers of the world with the causes, progress, and meaning of the Russian November Revolution, were put together. History willed it that the delegates of the most revolutionary regime the world has ever known had to sit at the same diplomatic table with the representatives of the most reactionary caste among all the ruling classes. At the sittings of the Peace Conference we did not for one moment forget that we were the representatives of a revolutionary class. We addressed our speeches to the war-weary workers of all countries. Our energies were sustained by the profound conviction that the final word in ending the war, as in all other questions, would be said by the European working class. When speaking to Kühlmann and Czernin, we all the time had in our mind's eye our friends and comrades, Karl Liebknecht and Fritz Adler. My own free time I devoted to

INTRODUCTION

preparing a pamphlet intended for the workers of Germany, Austria-Hungary, and of all other countries. The bourgeois Press of the whole of Europe is unanimous in its slanders and execrations of the proletarian regime in Russia. The Socialist " patriotic " Press, bereft of courage and of faith in its own work, has revealed a total incapacity to understand and to interpret to the working masses the meaning of the Russian Revolution. I want to come to their help by means of the present booklet. I believe that the revolutionary workers of Europe and of other parts of the world will understand us. I believe that they will, in the near future, start on the same work as we are now engaged in, but that, aided by their greater experience and their more perfect intellectual and technical means, they will perform this work more thoroughly, and will help us to overcome all difficulties.

L. TROTSKY.

BREST-LITOVSK,
February 12, 1918.

THE RUSSIAN REVOLUTION

EVENTS at the present time succeed one another so rapidly that it is difficult to reproduce them from memory even in their simple chronological order. I have no papers or documents at hand. At the same time the periodical breaks in the negotiations at Brest-Litovsk give me a certain amount of leisure which, under present conditions, is not likely to recur. I shall, therefore, try to sketch from memory the course and development of the November Revolution, reserving to myself the right to complete and correct my narrative at some future date, with the aid of documentary evidence.

What distinguished our party almost from the very first stage of the Revolution was the firm conviction that the logic of events would eventually place it in power. I am not speaking here of the theoreticians of our party, who, many years before the Revolution, even before the Revolution of 1905, had come to the conclusion, from a close analysis of the class relations in Russia, that the victorious course of a revolution would inevitably place the power of the State in the hands of the proletariat, supported by the wide masses of the poorest peasantry. The main foundation for this belief was the insignificance of the Russian middle-class democracy and the concentrated character of Russian industry, and, therefore, the immense social importance of the Russian working class. The insignificance of the Russian middle-class democracy is but the obverse side of the power and importance of the proletariat. True, the war temporarily deceived many people on this point, and, above all, it deceived the leading sections of middle-class democracy itself. The war assigned the decisive rôle in the Revolution to the army, and the old army was the peasantry.

Had the Revolution developed more normally, that is, in conditions of peace-time, such as prevailed in 1912, when it really began, the proletariat would inevitably have taken the leading rôle throughout, whilst the peasant masses would have been gradually towed along by the proletariat into the revolutionary whirlpool. But the war imparted an entirely different logic to the course of events. The army had organized the peasantry, not on a political, but on a military basis. Before the peasant masses found themselves united on a common platform of definite revolutionary demands and ideas, they had already become united in regiments, divisions, corps, and armies. The lower middle-class democrats, scattered throughout this army, and playing a leading part in it both in a military and intellectual sense, were almost entirely imbued with middle-class revolutionary sentiments. The deep social discontent of the masses grew ever deeper and strove for expression, particularly owing to the military *débâcle* of Tsardom. Immediately the Revolution broke out, the advanced sections of the proletariat revived the traditions of 1905 by calling upon the popular masses to organize in representative bodies, viz. the " Councils " of delegates (Soviets).

The army thus had to send representatives to revolutionary bodies before its political consciousness in any way corresponded to the level of the rapidly developing revolutionary events. Whom could the soldiers send as their representatives? Naturally, only those intellectuals and semi-intellectuals who were to be found in their midst and who possessed at least a minimum amount of political knowledge, and were capable of giving utterance to it. In this way, by the will of the awakening army, the lower middle-class intellectuals found themselves suddenly raised to a position of enormous influence. Doctors, engineers, lawyers, journalists, who in pre-war days had led a humdrum private life and laid no claim of any sort to political influence, became, overnight, representatives of whole corps and armies, and discovered that they were the " leaders " of the Revolution. The haziness of their political ideas fully corresponded to the formless state of the revolutionary consciousness of the masses themselves. They contemptuously looked down upon us as mere sectarians because we were urging the social demands of the working class and the peasants in a most resolute and uncompromising fashion. At the same time these lower middle-class democrats, in spite of their proud demeanour of revolutionary upstarts, felt a profound diffidence both in their own capacities and in the masses who had raised them to such an unexpectedly high place. Calling themselves Socialists and really regarding themselves as such, these intellectuals looked up to the political authority of the Liberal bourgeoisie, to its knowledge and its methods, with an ill-concealed respect. Hence the endeavour of the lower middle-class leaders to obtain, at all costs, the co-operation of the Liberal middle class by way of an alliance or coalition. The programme of the party of Socialist Revolutionaries, based as it all is on vague humanitarian formulæ, and employing general sentiments and moral constructions in the place of class-war methods, was the most suitable spiritual dress that could have been found for these improvised leaders. Their efforts to find some sort of support for their own intellectual and political helplessness in the impressive political and scientific knowledge of the bourgeoisie found a theoretical sanction in the teaching of the Mensheviks, who argued that the present Revolution was a bourgeois revolution, and could not, therefore, be carried through without the participation of the bourgeoisie in the Government. A natural *bloc* was thus formed

10

between the Socialist Revolutionaries and Mensheviks, expressing both the timid and hesitating
political mind of the middle-class intellectuals
and its vassal attitude towards Imperialist
Liberalism.

To us, it was perfectly clear that the logic of the
class struggle would sooner or later destroy this
temporary combination and fling aside the leaders
of this period of transition. The hegemony of
the lower middle-class intellectuals was at bottom
the expression of the fact that the peasantry,
suddenly called to take part in organized political
life through the machinery of the army, had by
sheer weight of numbers pushed aside and overwhelmed the proletariat for the time being. Even
more, in so far as the middle-class leaders had
been raised to a dizzy height by the powerful mass
of the army, the working class itself, with the
exception of its advanced sections, could not but
become imbued with a certain political respect
for them and try to maintain political contact
with them for fear of finding themselves divorced
from the peasantry. And this was a very serious
matter, for the older generation still remembered
the lesson of 1905, when the proletariat was
crushed, just because the massive peasant reserves
had not come up in time for the decisive battles.
That is why in the first phase of the new Revolution also the proletarian masses showed themselves highly accessible to the political ideology of
the Socialist Revolutionaries and the Mensheviks
—especially as the Revolution had aroused the

hitherto slumbering backward masses of workers, and thus made the hazy radicalism of the intellectuals a sort of preparatory school for them. The Council of Workers', Soldiers', and Peasants' Delegates meant in these conditions the predominance of peasant amorphousness over proletarian Socialism, and the predominance of intellectual Radicalism over the peasant amorphousness.

The structure of Soviets rose so rapidly to a gigantic height mainly because of the leading part played in their labours by the intellectuals, with their technical knowledge and middle-class connections. But to us it was perfectly clear that this grand structure was built on deep internal contradictions and would inevitably collapse at the next stage of the Revolution.

THE QUESTION OF WAR.

The Revolution grew directly out of the war, and the latter became the touchstone for all parties and forces of the Revolution. The intellectual leaders had been against the war. Many of them, while the Tsar was still on his throne, considered themselves as belonging to the left wing of the International, and were Zimmerwaldians. But everything changed immediately they felt themselves to be in "responsible" positions. To pursue a revolutionary Socialist policy would have meant in the circumstances a break with their own and the Entente bourgeoisie, but, as we have said, the political impotence of the middle-class intellectuals and semi-intellectuals led them to seek protection in an alliance with bourgeois Liberalism. Hence the pitiful and truly disgraceful rôle of the middle-class leaders in respect of the question of the war. They confined themselves to lamentations and rhetoric, and addressed secret exhortations and entreaties to the Allied Governments, while, in practice, they walked the same paths as the Liberal bourgeoisie. The soldiers in the trenches were, of course, unable to follow the argument that the war, in which they had fought for three years, had changed its character because certain new personalities, calling themselves Socialist Revolutionaries and Mensheviks, were taking part in the Government at Petrograd. Miliukoff had replaced the *tchinovnik* Pokrovsky, Terestchenko, then succeeded Miliukoff —that meant that bureaucratic perfidy was first replaced by militant Cadet Imperialism, then by unprincipled nebulousness and political servility,; but this did not result in any objective changes, and there seemed no way out of the terrible vicious circle of the war. In this lay the primary cause for the further dissolution of the army. The agitators had been telling the masses of soldiers that the Tsarist Government had been driving them to slaughter for no object or sense,; but those who replaced the Tsar were able neither to change the character of the war in any way nor to make a fight for peace.

During the first months of the Revolution there

had been a mere marking of time. This provoked the impatience alike of the army and of the Allied Governments. Hence the offensive of July 1st. It had been demanded by the Allies, who insisted that the old Tsarist bills must be honoured by the Revolution. Frightened at their own impotence and at the growing discontent of the masses, the lower middle-class leaders readily accepted these demands. They, indeed, began to think that an attack by the Russian Army was all that was wanted in order to attain peace. An offensive began to appear to them as a way out of the wilderness, as a means of solving the problem of the situation, as the one hope of salvation. It is difficult to imagine a more monstrous and more criminal illusion. At that time they spoke of the offensive in exactly the same terms in which the Social-Patriots of all countries had spoken at the beginning of the war about the necessity of supporting the cause of national defence, of strengthening the sacred unity of the nation, etc. All their Zimmerwaldian Internationalism vanished as by magic.

To us, who were in opposition, it was clear that the offensive was a terribly perilous step, that it might even endanger the whole Revolution. We warned all and sundry that the army, newly awakened and shaken as it was by the thunder of events which as yet it had only half understood, could not be sent into battle without previously imparting to it new ideas which it could assimilate. We warned, remonstrated, threatened. But

14

THE RUSSIAN REVOLUTION

the parties in power, bound as they were to the bourgeoisie, had no other way left open to them, and naturally treated us with enmity and implacable hatred.

THE CAMPAIGN AGAINST THE BOLSHEVIKS.

The future historian will be unable, without deep emotion, to look through the Russian papers for May and June 1917, when the minds of the people were being prepared for the offensive. Almost all the articles, without exception, in all the official and semi-official organs were directed against the Bolsheviks. There was scarcely a charge, scarcely a calumny, that was not levelled against us in that period. Of course, the leading rôle in this campaign was played by the Cadet bourgeoisie, whose class instinct led it to recognize that the question at issue was not merely the offensive, but the entire further course of the Revolution and, in the first place, the form of Government authority. The whole bourgeois machinery for manufacturing " public opinion " was put into motion at full steam. All the Government offices and institutions, publications, public platforms, and university chairs were drawn into the service of this one general aim: of making the Bolsheviks impossible as a political party. In this concentrated effort and in this dramatic newspaper campaign against the Bolsheviks were already contained the first germs of the civil war which was bound to accompany the next phase of the Revolution. The sole aim of all this incitement and slander was to create an impenetrable wall of estrangement and enmity between the labouring masses on the one hand and " educated Society " on the other.

The Liberal bourgeoisie understood that it could not win the support of the masses without the help of the lower middle-class democrats, who, as we pointed out above, had temporarily become the leaders of the revolutionary organizations. Consequently, the immediate aim of the political incitements against the Bolsheviks was to bring about an irreconcilable feeling of enmity between our party and the wide ranks of the Socialist intellectuals, who, having broken away from the proletariat, could not but fall into political bondage to the Liberal bourgeoisie.

It was during the first All-Russian Congress of the Soviets that the first alarming crash of thunder occurred, which warned of the coming storm. Our party had projected an armed demonstration at Petrograd for June 23rd. Its proximate object was to bring pressure to bear upon the Congress. " Take over the power in the State "—this it was that the Petrograd workers wanted to tell the Socialist Revolutionaries and Mensheviks who had come from all parts of the country. " Spurn the bourgeoisie ! Have done with the idea of coalition, and take the reins of power into your own hands ! " We were quite certain that if the Socialist Revolutionaries and Mensheviks broke with the Liberal bourgeoisie, they would be compelled to seek support from the most energetic and most advanced elements of the proletariat, which would thus obtain the leading rôle in the Revolution. But that was just what frightened the lower middle-class leaders. In conjunction with the Government, in which they had their own representatives, and shoulder to shoulder with the Liberal and counter-revolutionary bourgeoisie, they opened a truly savage campaign against the projected demonstration so soon as they got wind of it. Everything possible was set in motion against us. We were at that time a small minority at the Congress, and we gave way; the demonstration did not take place. But all the same it left a very deep mark in the minds of the two contending parties, and made the gulf between them deeper and their mutual antagonism more acute. At the closed sitting of the Presidential Bureau of the Congress, in which also representatives of the various parties took place, Tsereteli, then a member of the Coalition Government, speaking with all the resoluteness of a narrow-minded lower middle-class doctrinaire, declared that the only danger threatening the Revolution was the Bolsheviks and the Petrograd workers who had been armed by them. He therefore argued that the people " who did not know how to use arms " must be disarmed. Of course, he had in mind the Petrograd workers and that portion of the Petrograd garrison which supported our party. However, no disarming took place, as the political and psychological conditions were not yet ripe enough for such an extreme measure.

To compensate the masses for the loss of their demonstration, the Congress of the Soviets itself organized an unarmed demonstration on July 1st. And that day became the day of our political triumph. The masses turned out in overwhelming numbers, but although they came out in answer to the call of the official Soviet authority—a sort of counterblast to the miscarried demonstration of June 23rd—the workers and soldiers had inscribed on their banners and placards the demands and battle-cries of *our* party: " Down with the secret treaties ! " " Down with the policy of strategical offensives ! " " Long live an honourable peace ! " " Down with the ten capitalist Ministers ! " " All power for the Soviets ! " There were only three placards with expressions of confidence in the Coalition Government: one from a Cossack regiment, another from the Plekhanoff group, and a third from the Petrograd " Bund," an organization consisting largely of non-proletarian elements. This demonstration proved not only to our opponents, but also to ourselves, that we were far stronger in Petrograd than had been imagined.

THE OFFENSIVE OF JULY 1ST.

As a result of this demonstration of the revolutionary masses a Government crisis seemed inevitable. But the impression made by the

demonstration was wiped out by the news from
the front announcing that the revolutionary army
had taken the offensive. On the very same day
when the workers and garrison of Petrograd had
been demanding the publication of the secret
treaties and a public offer of peace, Kerensky
had thrown the revolutionary troops into the
offensive. This, of course, was no fortuitous
coincidence. Everything had been arranged
beforehand, and the moment for the offensive
had been chosen not on military, but on political
grounds. On July 2nd there was a series of
so-called patriotic demonstrations in the streets
of Petrograd. The Nevsky Prospekt, the main
bourgeois artery, was full of excited groups of
people, amongst which officers, journalists, and
well-dressed ladies were carrying on a bitter
campaign against the Bolsheviks.

The first news of the results of the offensive
was favourable, and the leading Liberal organs
considered that the chief task had been aecom-
plished—that the blow struck on July 1st, quite
apart from what might be its subsequent military
developments, would prove fatal to the further
progress of the Revolution. It would lead to
the re-establishment of the old army discipline
and strengthen the commanding position of the
Liberal bourgeoisie in the country. We, however, had predicted something else besides. In
a special declaration which we read out at the
first Congress of the Soviets a few days before
the offensive, we had stated that that offensive

would inevitably destroy the internal coherence of the army, that it would put different sections of it against one another, and that it would lend an enormous preponderance to the counter-revolutionary elements, since the maintenance of discipline in a shattered army, whose vigour had not been renewed by new ideals, would be impossible without the employment of brutal measures of repression. In other words, we had predicted in that declaration all those consequences which were subsequently comprised under the name of Kornilovism. We considered that the Revolution was running the greatest danger alike in the case of the offensive succeeding (which, however, we did not believe) and in the case of its failing, as we thought to be almost inevitable. The success of the offensive would have the effect of uniting the lower with the upper middle class in common chauvinistic aspirations, thus isolating the revolutionary proletariat, while its failure might lead to the complete collapse of the army, to a chaotic retreat, the loss of more provinces, and the disappointment and despair of the masses.

Events turned out in accordance with the second part of the alternative. The news of the victorious advance of the army did not continue long. It was succeeded by gloomy communications regarding the refusal of many sections of the army to support the attacking troops, the terrible losses among the officers, who sometimes alone formed shock battalions, and so on.

THE RUSSIAN REVOLUTION

The background to these military events was formed by growing difficulties in the internal life of the country. The Coalition Government had not made a single decisive step forward in the solution of the agrarian, industrial, or national questions. The food supply and transport were becoming more and more dislocated. Local conflicts became more and more frequent. The "Socialist" Ministers tried to persuade the masses to wait. All decisions and measures were being put off, including the convocation of the Constituent Assembly. The insolvency and instability of the regime were obvious. There were two possible ways out: either to hurl the bourgeoisie from power and allow the Revolution to go forward, or to "restrain" the masses by means of brutal repression. Kerensky and Tsereteli were pursuing a middle course, and only succeeded in making the confusion worse confounded. When once the Cadets, by far the cleverer and more far-seeing representatives in the Coalition, saw that the failure of the July offensive might strike a heavy blow not only at the Revolution, but also at the parties standing at the head of affairs, they hastened to step aside for the time being, thus throwing the whole weight of the responsibility on their colleagues of the Left. On July 15th a Ministerial crisis broke out, ostensibly over the Ukrainian question. This was altogether a moment of great political tension in every sense. Deputations and individual delegates arrived from different parts of the front, bearing the tale of the chaos which now reigned supreme in the army as a result of the offensive. The so-called Government Press demanded stern measures of repression. Similar demands commenced to appear more and more frequently in the so-called Socialist Press. Kerensky was more and more rapidly, or, rather, more and more openly, passing over to the side of the Cadets and the Cadet generals, ostentatiously displaying his enmity and, indeed, hatred towards the revolutionary parties in general. The Allied Embassies were exerting pressure on the Government, demanding the re-establishment of discipline and the continuation of the offensive. Confusion reigned supreme in Government circles, whilst the indignation of the workers grew apace and imperatively demanded some outlet. " Seize the opportunity of the resignation of the Cadet Ministers and assume complete control over the Government ": such was the call of the Petrograd workers on the leading Soviet parties, the Socialist Revolutionaries and the Mensheviks. I remember the sitting of the Executive Committee of July 15th. The Socialist Ministers reported on the new Government crisis. We waited with intense interest to hear what position they would take up now that the Government had ingloriously gone to pieces at the first serious test provoked by the Coalition policy itself. Tsereteli was the reporter. He explained to us very fully that the concessions he and Terestchenko had made to the Kieff Rada in no way meant the dismemberment of the country, and did not justify the action of the Cadets in leaving the Ministry. Tsereteli charged the Cadet leaders with being doctrinaires on the question of centralism, with a want of understanding of the need of a compromise with the Ukrainians, and so forth. The impression made by the reporter was really a pitiful one ! The hopeless doctrinaire of the Coalition accusing the Cadets of being doctrinaires—the Cadets, those sober-minded political champions of Capitalism, who had seized the first opportunity for making their political bailiffs pay the cost for the fateful turn which they had imparted to the course of events by the July offensive ! After all the experiences of the Coalition, it might have seemed that there could be only one way out, viz. to break with the Cadets and to form a purely Soviet Government. The correlation of forces inside the Soviets at the time was such that a Soviet Government would have meant, from a party point of view, the concentration of power in the hands of the Socialist Revolutionaries and Mensheviks. We were deliberately aiming at such a result, since the constant re-elections to the Soviets provided the necessary machinery for securing a sufficiently faithful reflection of the growing radicalization of the masses of the workers and soldiers. We foresaw that after the break of the Coalition with the bourgeoisie the radical tendencies would necessarily gain the upper hand on the Soviets. In such conditions the struggle of the proletariat for power would naturally shift to the floor of the Soviet organizations, and would proceed in a painless fashion. On their part, having broken with the bourgeoisie, the lower middle-class democrats would themselves become the target for its attacks, and would, therefore, be compelled to seek a closer alliance with the Socialist working class, and sooner or later their political amorphousness and irresolution would be overcome by the labouring masses under the influence of our criticism. This is why we urged the two leading Soviet parties to take the reins of power into their own hands, although we ourselves had no confidence in them, and frankly said so.

But even after the Ministerial crisis of July 15th, Tsereteli and those who thought with him did not give up their pet idea of a coalition. They explained to the Executive Committee that the chief Cadet leaders were, it was true, demoralized by doctrinairism and even by counter-revolutionary sympathies, but that in the provinces there were many bourgeois elements who would march side by side with the revolutionary democracy and whose co-operation would be secured by the co-option of some representatives of the upper middle class in the new Ministry. Dan was already placing high hopes on a new Radical-Democratic party which had been concocted about that time by a few doubtful politicians. The news that the Coalition had broken to pieces only to give rise to a new Coalition spread rapidly throughout Petrograd, and created a wave of dismay and indignation in the workers' and soldiers' quarters. This was the origin of the events of July 16th-18th.

THE JULY DAYS.

Already during the sitting of the Executive Committee we had been informed over the telephone that the machine-gun regiment was getting ready for a demonstration. We then took measures, also over the telephone, to restrain it₁; but important events were preparing underneath. Representatives of army units disbanded for insubordination were coming from the front with alarming accounts of repressions, which made the Petrograd garrison very uneasy. The discontent of the Petrograd workers with the official leaders was proving the more acute, as Tsereteli, Dan, and Tshkheidze were obviously bent on falsifying the sentiments of the proletariat by trying to prevent the Petrograd Soviet from giving expression to the new views of the labouring masses. The All-Russian Executive Committee, elected at the June Congress and depending for support on the more backward provinces, was pushing the Petrograd Soviet more and more to the background and was taking into its own hands even the conduct of purely Petrograd affairs. A conflict was inevitable. The workers and soldiers were exerting pressure from below, giving violent expression to their discontent with the official policy of the Soviet, and demanded from our party more drastic action. We considered that in view of the still backward condition of the provinces the hour for such action had not yet struck ; but at the same time we feared lest the events at the front might produce an immense confusion in the ranks of the revolutionary workers and create despair among them.

In the ranks of our party, the attitude towards the events of July 16th-18th was perfectly definite. On the one hand, there was the fear that Petrograd might become isolated from the more backward provinces ; on the other hand, there was the hope that an active and energetic intervention of Petrograd might save the situation. The party propagandists in the lower ranks went hand in hand with the masses and carried on an uncompromising agitation.

There was still some hope that a demonstration of the revolutionary masses might break down the obstinate doctrinairism of the Coalitionists and compel them to realize at last that they could only maintain themselves in power if they completely broke with the bourgeoisie. Contrary to what was said and written at the time in the bourgeois Press, there was no intention whatever in our party of seizing the reins of power by means of an armed rising. It was only a revolutionary demonstration which broke out spontaneously, though guided by us politically. The Central Executive Committee was sitting at the Taurida Palace when the stormy waves of armed soldiers and workers surrounded the Palace on every side. Among the demonstrators there was, undoubtedly, an insignificant minority of Anarchists who were ready to use arms against the Soviet Centre. There were also some, obviously hired, Black Hundred elements who tried to seize the occasion for causing a riot and pogroms. It was from these elements that demands emanated for the arrest of Tchernoff and Tsereteli, for the forcible suppression of the Central Committee, etc. There was even an actual attempt made to arrest Tchernoff. Subsequently, at Kresty Prison, I met a sailor who had taken part in that attempt. He turned out to have been an ordinary criminal and had been imprisoned at the Kresky for burglary. But the bourgeois and compromise-mongers' Press had described the whole movement as being merely of a pogrom and counter-revolutionary character, and yet, at the same time, as a Bolshevik manœuvre, having as its direct object the seizure of power by armed coercion of the Central Executive Committee.

The movement of July 16th-18th showed with perfect clearness that the leading parties of the Soviet lived in Petrograd in a complete political vacuum. It is true that the garrison was by no means entirely with us at that time. There were among it units which still hesitated, were still undecided and passive. But apart from the ensigns, there was not a single unit among the garrison, which was willing to fight against us in defence of the Government or the leading parties in the Soviet. It was from the front that troops had to be fetched. The entire strategy of Tsereteli, Tchernoff, and others, during those July days was to gain time so as to enable Kerensky to draw " reliable " troops into Petrograd. Delegation after delegation entered the Taurida Palace, which was surrounded by a huge armed crowd, and demanded a complete break with the bourgeoisie, energetic measures of social reform, and the commencement of peace negotiations. We, Bolsheviks, met every new detachment of demonstrators, either in the street or in the Palace, with harangues, calling on them to be calm, and assuring them that with the masses in their present mood the compromise-mongers would be unable to form a new Coalition Ministry. The men of Kronstadt were particularly determined, and it was only with difficulty that we could keep them within the bounds of a bare demonstration. On July 17th the demonstration assumed a still more formidable character—this time under the direct leadership of our party. The Soviet leaders seemed to have lost their heads; their speeches were of an evasive character ; the answers given by Tchkheidze, the Ulysses, to the delegations were bereft of all political sense. It was clear that the political leaders were but marking time.

On the night of July 17th "trustworthy" troops commenced to arrive from the front. During the sitting of the Executive Committee, the Taurida Palace was suddenly filled with the brass notes of the "Marseillaise." The faces of the members of the Presidential Bureau changed immediately. Confidence, which had been so conspicuously lacking during the last few days, once more made its appearance. It was the Volhynian Regiment of the Guards which had arrived, the same regiment which a few months later marched at the head of the November Revolution under our banners.

From that moment everything changed. There was no longer any need to stand on ceremony with the delegations of workers and soldiers or the representatives of the Baltic Fleet. Speeches were delivered from the tribune of the Executive Committee about an armed "rebellion" which had now been "suppressed" by the faithful revolutionary troops. The Bolsheviks were declared to be a counter-revolutionary party.

The fright which the bourgeoisie had undergone during the two days of armed demonstration now became transformed into a raging hate which was displayed not only in the columns of their papers, but also in the streets of Petrograd, especially on the Nevsky Prospekt, where individual workers and soldiers were mercilessly beaten when caught carrying on their " criminal " agitation. Ensigns, officers, members of shock battalions, Knights of St. George, became masters of the situation, and rabid counter-revolutionaries placed themselves at their head. A ruthless suppression of workers' organizations and of institutions of our party was carried out throughout the city. There were arrests, raids, physical ill-treatment, and individual murders. In the night of July 17th-18th the then Minister of Justice, Pereverzeff, issued to the Press " documents " purporting to prove that at the head of the Bolshevik party there stood paid agents of Germany.

The leaders of the Socialist Revolutionary and Menshevik parties had known us too long and too well to believe this accusation, but at the same time they were too closely interested in its success against us to protest against it publicly. Even now one cannot recall, without disgust, the orgy of lies poured forth in the columns of all the bourgeois and Coalitionist Press. Our papers were suppressed. Revolutionary Petrograd then felt that the provinces and the army were as yet far from being with it. For a brief moment the workers were stricken with dismay. In the Petrograd garrison the disbanded regiments were sternly repressed, and individual units were disarmed. All this time the Soviet leaders were busy fabricating a new Ministry to include third-rate middle-class groups which, without in any way strengthening the Government, only deprived it of the last vestiges of revolutionary initiative.

In the meantime, events at the front were taking their course. The whole army had been shaken to its foundation. The soldiers saw that the vast majority of the officers who had camouflaged themselves at the beginning of the Revolution were, in reality, deeply hostile to the new regime. At the Main Headquarters there was now going on quite openly a selection of counter-revolutionary elements. The Bolshevik publications were ruthlessly persecuted. The offensive had long ago given way to a tragic retreat. The bourgeois Press was savagely slandering the army, and although on the eve of the offensive the governing parties had declared that we were an insignificant handful, that the army knew nothing of us and cared less, now that their adventure of the offensive had ended so tragically, these same people and parties were throwing the whole responsibility for the failure on us. The prisons were packed to overflowing with revolutionary soldiers and workers. For the investigation of the affair of July 16th-18th all the old wolves of Tsarist judiciary were re-called ; yet the Socialist Revolutionaries and Mensheviks dared demand of Lenin, Zinovieff, and other comrades that they should voluntarily give themselves up to " justice " !

AFTER THE JULY DAYS.

The feeling of dismay in the workers' quarters soon passed, and gave way to a new wave of revolutionary enthusiasm, not only among the proletariat, but even among the Petrograd garrison. The Coalitionists were losing all in-fluence, and the wave of Bolshevism commenced to spread throughout the country and penetrated, in spite of all obstacles, even into the army.

The new Coalition Ministry, with Kerensky at

its head, now openly entered on the path of repressions. The Ministry re-established the death penalty for soldiers, our papers were put down and our propagandists were arrested. But all this only increased our influence. In spite of all hindrances placed in the way of re-elections to the Petrograd Soviet, the relative strength of the parties had altered to such an extent that on many important questions we were already in a majority. Exactly the same happened in the Moscow Soviet. At that time, in company with many other comrades, I was already in prison at Kresty, having been arrested for taking part in the agitation and organization of the armed rising of July 16th-18th in agreement with the German Government and with the object of aiding the military plans of the Hohenzollerns. The well-known examining magistrate of the Tsarist regime, Alexandroff, who had conducted several prosecutions against revolutionaries, now received the mission to protect the Republic against the counter-revolutionary Bolsheviks. Under the old regime prisoners used to be divided into political and criminal ; now a new terminology was introduced: criminals and Bolsheviks. Amongst the arrested soldiers bitter perplexity reigned. Young men from the villages who had never before taken part in politics, but who had thought that the Revolution had made them free once for all, now stared with amazement at the bolted doors and the grated windows. During our walks in the courtyard they anxiously asked me each time what it all meant and how it would all end. I comforted them by saying that we should come out victorious in the end.

KORNILOFF'S RISING.

The end of August was marked by the rising of General Korniloff. It was the immediate result of the mobilisation of the counter-revolutionary forces, to which the offensive of July had given a great impetus. At the celebrated State Conference at Moscow in the latter half of August, Kerensky tried to take up a position midway between the propertied classes and lower middle-class democrats. The Bolsheviks were regarded as standing altogether outside the law. Kerensky threatened them with " blood and iron " amidst a storm of applause from the propertied sections of the Conference and the traitorous silence of the lower middle-class democrats. But Kerensky's hysterical cries and threats did not satisfy the leaders of the counter-revolutionary cause. They saw only too well the revolutionary wave that was spreading throughout the country, enveloping the workers, the peasants, and the army, and they considered it imperative to employ immediately the most extreme measures in order to teach the masses an unforgettable lesson. In agreement with the propertied bourgeoisie, which saw in him its hero, Korniloff took this risky matter on his shoulders. Kerensky, Savinkoff, Filonenko, and other Socialist Revolutionaries in or about office took part in 'bis plot, but all of them betrayed Korniloff as soon as they saw that if he should come out victorious they themselves would be thrown overboard. I lived through the episode in prison and followed it up in the papers: free access to the papers was the only important difference between Kerensky's prison regime and the old one. The adventure of the Cossack General fell through; in six months of the Revolution the masses had developed sufficient spirit and strength of organization to repel any open counter-revolutionary attack. The Coalitionist Soviet parties were frightened to the last degree by the possible developments of the Korniloff plot, which threatened to sweep away not only the Bolsheviks, but the whole of the Revolution, together with its leading parties. The Socialist Revolutionaries and the Mensheviks then set out to "legalize" the position of the Bolsheviks, but only by half and with numerous reservations, scenting possible dangers in the future. The same Kronstadt sailors who, after the July occurrence, had been branded as hooligans and counter-revolutionaries, were now summoned to Petrograd to defend the Revolution against the Korniloff danger. They came without demur, without taunts, without any reminders of the past, and took up the most responsible positions. I had then a perfect right to remind Tsereteli of the words I had thrown at him in May when he was abusing the men of Kronstadt: "When a counter-revolutionary general tries to tie a knot round the throat of the Revolution, the Cadets will be soaping the rope and the Kronstadt sailors will come to help us and to die with us."

The Soviet organizations displayed everywhere at the rear and at the front their vitality and strength in the fight against the Korniloff rising. Scarcely anywhere did matters come to actual fighting. The revolutionary masses simply paralysed the General's plot. Just as in July the Coalitionists could find no soldiers to fight against us among the Petrograd garrison, so now Korniloff could find no soldiers at the front to fight against the Revolution. He could only act at all by deceit, and the efforts of the propagandists soon put an end to his designs.

Judging by the papers, I hoped for a very rapid development of events and for an early passing of the Government authority into the hands of the Soviets. The growth of the influence and strength of the Bolsheviks was undoubted, and it had now received an irresistible impetus. The Bolsheviks had warned against the Coalition, against the July offensive, and had foretold the Korniloff rebellion. The popular masses could now see that we had been right. At the most anxious moments of the Korniloff plot, when the Caucasian " Savage " Division was marching on Petrograd, the Petrograd Soviet, with the unwilling connivance of the Government, had armed the workers. The regiments which had been summoned against us had long ago become transformed in the hot atmosphere of Petrograd, and were now entirely on our side. The Korniloff attempt was bound finally to open the eyes of the army to the inadmissibility of any further understanding with the bourgeois counter-revolutionaries. One might, therefore, well have expected that the suppression of the Korniloff attempt would be followed by an immediate effort of the revolutionary forces, guided by our party, to obtain power. But events developed more slowly. In spite of the intensity of revolutionary feeling, the masses had become more wary since the severe lesson of the July days, and forswore all spontaneous action, waiting for a direct call and guidance from their leaders. But the leaders of our party, too, were in a waiting mood. In these circumstances the winding up of the Korniloff adventure, although it had fundamentally altered the correlation of forces in our favour, did not lead to any immediate political changes.

THE STRUGGLE WITHIN THE SOVIETS.

By that time the predominance of our party in the Petrograd Soviet became definite. This was made evident in a dramatic form in connection with the question of the constitution of the Presidential Bureau. At the time when the Socialist Revolutionaries and the Mensheviks reigned supreme in the Soviets, they tried all they could to isolate the Bolsheviks. Even when we had at least one-third of the total seats on the Petrograd Soviet, they would not admit a single representative of our party to the Presidential Bureau. After the Petrograd Soviet had passed a resolution in favour of a purely Soviet Government by a somewhat precarious majority, our group demanded the constitution of a Coalition Presidency on the basis of proportional representation. The old Bureau, which included Tchkheidze, Tsereteli, Kerensky, Skobeleff, and Tchernoff, would not hear of this. It is worth while remembering this just now, when the other parties talk of the need of a " united democratic front " and accuse us of exclusiveness. A special meeting of the Petrograd Soviet was called to decide the constitution of the Bureau. Both sides mobilized all their forces and reserves for this struggle. Tsereteli came out with a programmatic speech and argued that the question of the Presidential Bureau was really a question of policy. We thought we should get a little less than half of the votes, and were prepared to consider this as a success. To our own great surprise the voting by roll-call showed more than a hundred majority in our favour. " During six months," said Tsereteli, " we stood at the head of the Petrograd Soviet and led it from victory to victory. We hope that you will at least remain half that time at the posts you are about to take up." A similar change of the directing parties took place in the Moscow Soviet. The provincial Soviets, too, passed one after the other into the hands of the Bolsheviks. The time was getting near for the

summoning of an All-Russian Congress of
Soviets. But the leading group of the Central
Executive Committee was trying all it could to
put the Congress off to the dim and distant future,
in the hope of making it altogether impossible.
It was evident that the new Congress would give
our party a majority, would elect a new Central
Executive Committee corresponding to the new
orientation of the parties, and would rob the
Coalitionists of their most important strong-
hold. The struggle for the calling together
of the All-Russian Congress of the Soviets
thus became a matter of the greatest importance
to us.

As against this, the Mensheviks and Socialist
Revolutionaries made a proposal for the calling
together of a Democratic Conference. This body,
they thought, they would be able to play off
both against us and against Kerensky.

The head of the Government had by this time
taken up quite an independent and irresponsible
position. He had been raised to power in the
first period of the Revolution by the Petrograd
Soviet. Kerensky had entered the Ministry in
the first instance without any provisional decision
of the Soviet, but the latter subsequently approved of the step. After the first Congress of
the Soviets the Socialist Ministers were considered
to be responsible to the Central Executive Committee. Their Cadet allies were only answerable
to their own party. After the July days the
Central Executive Committee, meeting the wishes

of the bourgeoisie, freed the Socialist Ministers from their responsibility to the Soviets, for the purpose, as it was alleged at the time, of creating a revolutionary dictatorship. This also is worth while remembering just now, when the very same people who were concocting the dictatorship of a small circle are now hurling charges and slanders against the dictatorship of a class.

The Moscow State Conference, at which the artificially selected propertied and democratic representatives balanced one another, had had for its chief aim the consolidation of Kerensky's power over the classes and parties. This aim had only been attained in appearance. In reality the Moscow Conference only revealed Kerensky's complete impotence, for he was almost equally a stranger to the propertied elements and to the lower middle-class democracy. But as the Liberals and the Conservatives applauded his tirades against the democracy, while the Coalitionists gave him a great ovation when he very guardedly disowned the counter-revolutionaries, he gained the impression that he was supported by both sides and disposed of unlimited authority. He threatened the workers and the revolutionary soldiers with blood and iron. His policy went still further along the road of conspiracies with Korniloff, which compromised him in the eyes of the Coalitionists. Tsereteli, in his characteristically vague diplomatic phrases, spoke of " personal " factors in politics and the necessity of circumscribing them. It was this task that the .

Democratic Conference had to discharge, composed as it was of representatives of the Soviets, Municipal Councils, Zemstvos, trade unions and co-operative societies—all selected in an arbitrary manner. The chief problem, however, was to provide for a sufficiently Conservative complexion of the Conference, to dissolve the Soviets once for all in the amorphous mass of democracy, and to consolidate their own power by means of this new organization against the tide of Bolshevism.

It will not be out of place here to note in a few words the difference between the political rôle of the Soviets and the democratic organs of self-government. Philistines have more than once pointed out to us that the new Municipal Councils and Zemstvos elected by universal suffrage are incomparably more democratic than the Soviets, and possess a more valid right to represent the whole population. This formal democratic criterion, however, has no real meaning in revolutionary times. Revolution is distinguished by this: that the consciousness of the masses undergoes rapid changes. New sections of the population constantly gain experience, revise their views of yesterday, work out new ones, reject old leaders, follow others, and press ever forward. In times of Revolution the (formally) democratic organizations, based on the ponderous mechanism of universal suffrage, inevitably lag behind the development of the political views of the masses. Not so the Soviets.

They depend directly on organic groups, such as workshops, factories, mines, companies, regiments, etc. In these cases, of course, there are no such legal guarantees for the perfect accuracy of the elections as in those to Municipal Councils and Zemstvos, but there is the far more important guarantee of the direct and immediate contact of the deputy with his electors. The member of the Town Council or Zemstvo depends on an amorphous mass of electors who invest him with authority for one year, and then dissolve. The Soviet electors, on the other hand, remain in permanent contact with one another by the very conditions of their life and work; their deputy is always under their direct observation and may at any moment be given new instructions, and, if necessary, may be censured, recalled, and replaced by somebody else.

As the general political evolution of the preceding months of the Revolution had been marked by the growing influence of the Bolsheviks at the expense of the Coalitionist parties, it was quite natural that this process should have been reflected most clearly and fully on the Soviets; the Town Councils and Zemstvos, in spite of all their formal democratic character, expressing not so much the sentiments of the masses today as those of yesterday. This explains the gravitation towards the Town Councils and Zemstvos on the part of those parties which have been losing ever more and more their footing in the revolutionary class. This question will again crop up, only on a larger scale, when we come to the Constituent Assembly.

THE DEMOCRATIC CONFERENCE.

The Democratic Conference, called together by Tsereteli and his coadjutors towards the end of September, was of an entirely artificial character, consisting, as it did, of a combination of representatives of Soviets with those of the organs of local self-government in such a proportion as to give a preponderance to the Coalitionist parties. The offspring of helplessness and confusion, the Conference ended in a pitiful fiasco. The propertied bourgeoisie regarded it with the greatest animosity, seeing in it an attempt to drive it from the position to which it had advanced at the Moscow gathering. On the other hand, the revolutionary working class and the masses of the peasantry and soldiers had condemned in advance the methods of adulteration used in calling the Conference together. The immediate task of the Coalitionists was to form a " responsible " Ministry. But even this was not attained. Kerensky did not want and would not allow any principle of responsibility, because the bourgeoisie at his back would not allow it. Non-responsibility before the organs of the so-called democracy meant, in effect, responsibility before the Cadets and the Allied Embassies. For the present this was sufficient for the bourgeoisie. On the question of coalition, the Conference revealed its complete insolvency. The number of votes cast for the principle of a coalition with the bourgeoisie was only little more than that cast against all coalitions, and a majority of votes was cast against a coalition with the Cadets. But with the exception of the latter, there were no parties among the bourgeoisie worth mentioning with whom a coalition could be entered into. Tsereteli fully explained this to the assembly. If the assembly did not understand this, so much the worse for it! And so behind the back of the Conference pourparlers were carried on unabashed with the very Cadets whom it had rejected, it having been decided that the Cadets should be treated not as Cadets, but as —public men! Pressed from the right and from the left, the lower middle-class democrats submitted to all this mockery of themselves and thereby demonstrated their complete political impotence.

A Council was elected from the Democratic Conference, which it was decided should be completed by the addition of some representatives of the propertied classes; and this " Provisional Parliament " was to fill the gap until the meeting of the Constituent Assembly. The new Coalition Ministry, contrary to Tsereteli's original plan, but in entire accordance with the plans of the bourgeoisie, was to maintain its formal independence as against the Provisional Parliament. The whole proceeding gave the impression of a pitiful and impotent product of a mind divorced from life, behind which could clearly be seen the complete capitulation of the lower middle-class democrats to that same propertied Liberal bourgeoisie which only a month before had openly supported Korniloff's attempt against the Revolution. The whole thing, then, amounted practically to the re-establishment and the perpetuation of the coalition with the Liberal bourgeoisie. There could no longer be any doubt that, quite independent of the composition of the future Constituent Assembly, the Government power would be in the hands of the bourgeoisie, since the Coalitionist parties, in spite of all the preponderance secured to them by the popular masses, were unalterably bent on a coalition with the Cadets, considering it impossible to form any Government without the aid of the bourgeoisie. The popular masses regarded Miliukoff's party with the greatest hostility. At all elections in the course of the Revolution the Cadets invariably suffered severe defeats; yet the very same parties, the Socialist Revolutionaries and Mensheviks, who smote the Cadet party at the elections hip and thigh, would, after the elections, invariably reserve for them a place of honour in the Coalition Cabinet. It was natural in these circumstances that the masses began to perceive more and more clearly that the Coalitionist parties were in reality playing the rôle of bailiffs and office-holders for the Liberal bourgeoisie.

THE RUSSIAN REVOLUTION

Meanwhile the internal situation was deteriorating and becoming more and more complicated. The war was dragging along without aim, without sense, without any perspective. The Government was taking no steps to extricate itself from the vicious circle. The ridiculous plan was put forward of sending Skobeleff to Paris in order to influence the Allied Imperialists, but no sensible person attached to it any serious importance. Korniloff surrendered Riga to the Germans in order to terrorize public opinion and so to gain a favourable opportunity for establishing an iron discipline in the army. Petrograd was threatened, and the middle-class elements were welcoming the danger with evident malignancy. Rodzianko, the former President of the Duma, openly said that the surrender of demoralized Petrograd to the Germans would constitute no great misfortune. He referred to the case of Riga, where, following upon the entry of the Germans, the Soviets were dissolved and strict order was established with the help of the old police. True, the Baltic Fleet would be lost; but the fleet had been demoralized by revolutionary propaganda, and the loss would, therefore, not be so very great. This cynicism of the garrulous *grand seigneur* expressed the secret thoughts of wide circles of the bourgeoisie. The handing over of Petrograd to the Germans would not really mean its final loss. By the peace treaty

45

Petrograd would be returned, but it would in the interval have been disciplined by German militarism. The Revolution in the meantime would be decapitated, and could therefore be more easily grappled with. Kerensky's Government had, in fact, no serious intention of defending the capital, and public opinion was being prepared for its possible surrender. Government offices were being transferred from Petrograd to Moscow and other towns.

It was in such circumstances that the Soldiers' Section of the Petrograd Soviet met at a full session. The general feeling was tense and agitated. If the Government was unable to defend Petrograd, let it conclude peace. And if it was incapable of concluding peace, let it clear out. This was how the Soldiers' Section expressed their views of the condition of affairs. This was the first signal of the coming November Revolution.

At the front the position of affairs was going from bad to worse. A cold autumn, wet and muddy, was drawing near. There was the prospect of a fourth winter campaign. The food supply was becoming worse every day. In the rear they had forgotten about the front. There were no reliefs, no reinforcements, and no warm clothing. The number of deserters was increasing daily. The old army committees, elected at the beginning of the Revolution, still remained in their places and supported Kerensky's policy. Re-elections were prohibited. An abyss

was formed between the army committees and
the masses of the army, and finally the soldiers
began to detest the committees. Again and again
delegates from the trenches would arrive at Petrograd and ask point-blank, at the sittings of the
Soviet : " What are we to do now? Who will
end the war, and how shall it be done? Why
is the Petrograd Soviet silent? "

THE INEVITABLE STRUGGLE FOR POWER.

The Petrograd Soviet was not silent. It
demanded the immediate assumption of authority
by the central and local Soviets, the immediate
transference of the land to the peasants, the
establishment of control by the workers over
industry, and the immediate initiation of peace
negotiations. So long as we had been in opposition, the cry " All power to the Soviets ! " was
a battle-cry of propaganda, but since we became
a majority on all the chief Soviets it imposed upon
us the duty of taking up an immediate and
direct struggle for power.

In the villages the position of affairs had
become complicated and confused to the last
degree. The Revolution had promised the
land to the peasants, but had forbidden the
latter to touch the land till the meeting of the
Constituent Assembly. The peasants at first
waited patiently; but when they began to lose
patience the Coalition Government resorted to
measures of repression. In the meantime the
prospect of the meeting of the Constituent

Assembly was becoming dimmer and dimmer.
The bourgeoisie was insisting that the Constituent
Assembly should not be summoned until after
the conclusion of peace. The peasant masses,
on the other hand, were becoming more and
more impatient, and what we had predicted at
the beginning of the Revolution was now coming
true. The peasant masses began to grab the
land on their own authority. Reprisals became
more frequent and severe, and the revolutionary land committees began to be arrested
—here and there. In some districts Kerensky
even proclaimed martial law. Delegates from
the villages began to stream to Petrograd, and
complained to the Soviet that they were
being arrested while trying to carry out the programme of the Soviets and handing over the
estates of the private landowners to the peasants'
committees. The peasants demanded our protection. We replied that we could only help them
if the government power were in our hands. Hence
it followed that if the Soviets did not want to become mere talking-shops they were bound to make
an effort to get the power into their own hands.

It was absurd to fight for the authority of the
Soviets six or eight weeks before the meeting
of the Constituent Assembly—so we were told by
the friends on the Right. But we were not in
the least infected by this fetishism of the Constituent Assembly. In the first place, there were
no guarantees that it would really be summoned.
The break-up of the army, the wholesale deser-

tions, the disorganization of the food supply, the agrarian revolution—all went to create an atmosphere but little favourable to the holding of elections to the Assembly. Moreover, the possible surrender of Petrograd 'to the Germans threatened to make such elections altogether impossible. In the second place, even if the Constituent Assembly were to be summoned under the direction of the old parties, on the old party lists, it could only become a protection for, and a confirmation of, the coalition principle of government. Neither the Socialist Revolutionaries nor the Mensheviks were capable of assuming authority without the help of the bourgeoisie. Only a revolutionary class could break the vicious circle in which the Revolution was floundering and disintegrating. It was essential that the authority should be snatched from the hands of those elements which directly or indirectly were serving the interests of the bourgeoisie and used the Government machinery for obstructing the revolutionary demands of the people.

THE STRUGGLE FOR THE SOVIET CONGRESS.

All power to the Soviets: such was the demand of our party. In the preceding period this meant, in terms of party divisions, complete authority for the Socialist Revolutionaries and Mensheviks as against the coalition with the Liberal bourgeoisie. Now, however, in November 1917, this demand meant the complete supremacy of the

revolutionary proletariat, headed now by the Bolshevik party. The question at issue was the
dictatorship of the working class, which was leading, or, to be more correct, was capable of
leading, the millions of the poorest peasantry.
This was the historical meaning of the November
rising.

Everything conspired to lead the party along
this path. From the very first days of the
Revolution we had insisted on the need and the
inevitability of the assumption of the entire
government authority by the Soviets. The
majority of the Soviets, after an intense internal
struggle, adopted our standpoint and took up this
demand. We were getting ready for the second
All-Russian Congress of the Soviets, at which
we expected a complete victory for our party.
The Central Executive Committee, on the other
hand, under the direction of Dan (the cautious
Tshkheidze left for the Caucasus in good time)
did everything possible to hinder the meeting
of the Soviet Congress. After great efforts,
supported by the Soviet group at the Democratic
Conference, we at last obtained the fixing of a
definite date for the Congress : November 7th.
This date has now become the greatest date in
Russian history. As a preliminary, we called
together in Petrograd a conference of the Soviets
of the Northern Provinces, including also the
Baltic Fleet and the Moscow Soviet. We had
a definite majority at this conference. We also
obtained some protection on the right flank from.

the left wing of the Socialist Revolutionaries, and laid the foundation for the business-like organization of the November rising.

THE CONFLICT OVER THE PETROGRAD GARRISON.

But even before that, before the conference of the Northern Soviets, something happened which was destined to play a most important part in the coming political struggle.

In the middle of October there appeared at a sitting of the Executive Committee the Soviet representative attached to the staff of the Petrograd military district, who informed us that the Main Headquarters were demanding the despatch of two-thirds of the Petrograd garrison to the front. What for? For the defence of Petrograd! The despatch was not to take place immediately, but it was necessary to get ready for it at once. The Staff asked the Petrograd Soviet to approve of this plan. We pricked up our ears. Already at the end of August five revolutionary regiments had been, wholly or in part, removed from Petrograd. This had been done on the demand of the then Commander-in-Chief, Korniloff, who at that very time was preparing to throw the Caucasian "Savage" Division against Petrograd with the object of settling with the revolutionary capital once and for all. We had thus already had the experience of a purely political redistribution of troops, carried out on the pretext of military operations.

It may be noted here, by way of anticipation, that documents which fell into our hands after the November Revolution showed, without any possibility of doubt, that the proposed evacuation of the Petrograd garrison in reality had absolutely nothing to do with military operations, and was forced on the Commander-in-Chief, Dukhonin, against his will by no other than Kerensky himself, who was anxious to clear Petrograd of the most revolutionary soldiers, that is, of those most hostile to himself.

But this was not known in the middle of October, and our suspicions were met by a storm of patriotic indignation. The military Staff tried to hurry us on, and Kerensky was impatient, as the ground beneath his feet was fast becoming too hot for him. We, however, did not hurry to answer. Certainly, Petrograd was in danger, and the terrible question of the defence of the capital exercised us greatly. But after the experience of the Korniloff days, after Rodzianko's words regarding salvation by a German occupation of Petrograd, how could we be assured that Petrograd would not be wilfully surrendered to the Germans as a punishment for its rebellious spirit? The Executive Committee refused to give its signature to the demand for the removal of two-thirds of the Petrograd garrison without examination. We declared that we must have proof of the reality of the military need which dictated the demand, and for that purpose some organization to examine the question must be created.   Thus arose the idea of establishing, side by side with the Soldiers' Section of the Soviets, that is, with the political representation of the garrison, a purely operative organ in the form of the Military Revolutionary Committee which ultimately acquired enormous power and became practically the instrument of the November Revolution.

Undoubtedly, already at that time, when we were proposing the creation of an organ to concentrate in its hands all the threads of the purely military direction of the Petrograd garrison, we were clearly realizing that this organ might become an invaluable revolutionary weapon. We were already at that time deliberately and openly steering for a rising and organizing ourselves for it. The opening of the All-Russian Congress of Soviets was fixed, as we said before, for November 7th, and there could be no longer any doubt that it would declare in favour of the assumption of supreme authority by the Soviets. But such a decision would have to be carried out at once, otherwise it would simply become a worthless platonic demonstration. It would have been in accord with the logic of the situation if we had fixed our rising for November 7th. The bourgeois Press, indeed, took this for granted'. But the fate of the Congress depended, in the first instance, on the Petrograd garrison. Would it allow Kerensky to surround the Congress and to break it up with the help of a few hundreds or thousands

of ensigns, cadets, and members of shock battalions? The very attempt to get the garrison
out of Petrograd—did it not signify that the
Government was preparing to break up the Congress of the Soviets? It would have been strange
indeed if it were not, seeing that we were
mobilizing quite openly, in face of the whole
country, all the strength of the Soviets for the
purpose of dealing the Coalition Government a
mortal blow.

And so the whole conflict in Petrograd was
coming to an issue over the question of the fate
of its garrison. In the first place, of course, it
affected the soldiers, but the workers, too, evinced
the liveliest interest in it, as they feared that on
the removal of the troops they might be crushed
by the military cadets and Cossacks. The conflict was thus assuming a very acute character,
and the question over which it was tending to
an issue was very unfavourable to the Kerensky
Government.

Parallel with this struggle over the garrison
was also going on the previously mentioned
struggle for the summoning of the Soviet
Congress, in connection with which we were proclaiming openly, in the name of the Petrograd
Soviet and the conference of the Soviets of the
Northern District, that the second Soviet Congress must dismiss the Kerensky Government and
become the real master of Russia. Practically
the rising was already proceeding, and was
developing in the face of the whole country.

During October the question of the rising played also an important part in the internal life of our party. Lenin, who was in hiding in Finland, wrote numerous letters insisting on more energetic tactics. Amongst the rank and file there was great fermentation and growing discontent, because the Bolshevik Party, now in a majority in the Soviets, was not putting its own battle-cries into practice. On October 28th a secret meeting of the Central Committee of our party took place, at which Lenin was present. On the order of the day was the question of the rising. With only two dissentients it was unanimously decided that the only means of saving the Revolution and the country from complete destruction was an armed rising, which must have for its object the conquest of supreme government authority by the Soviets.

THE DEMOCRATIC COUNCIL AND THE PROVISIONAL PARLIAMENT.

The Democratic Council which arose out of the Democratic Conference inherited all the impotence of the latter. The old Soviet parties, the Socialist Revolutionaries and the Mensheviks, had secured for themselves an artificial majority on the Council, apparently for the purpose of exposing still more thoroughly their entire political prostration. Behind the scenes Tsereteli was carrying on intricate negotiations with Kerensky and the representatives of the " propertied elements," as they began terming them in the

Council in order to avoid the " insulting " term
" bourgeoisie." Tsereteli's report on the progress and results of these negotiations sounded
very much like a funeral oration over the grave
of a whole revolutionary period. It turned out
that neither Kerensky nor the propertied elements
would agree to the principle of Ministerial responsibility to the new semi-representative body. On
the other hand; it was impossible to find " business-like " public men outside the Cadet Party.
The organizers of the business had to give in on
both points, which capitulation was so much the
more delightful as the Democratic Conference
had been called together specially for the purpose
of putting an end to the irresponsible regime,
the Conference, moreover, explicitly rejecting all
coalition with the Cadets. At the last few meetings of the Democratic Council before the
new Revolution there was a general atmosphere
of great tension and practical impotence. The
Council reflected not the progress of the Revolution, but the dissolution of parties whom the
Revolution had left far behind.

Already during the session of the Democratic
Conference I had raised the question in our party
of making a demonstrative exit from the Conference and of boycotting the Democratic
Council. It was necessary to demonstrate to the
masses by our action that the Coalitionists had
brought the Revolution into an impasse. The
struggle for the formation of a Soviet Government could only be carried on by revolutionary

methods. It was imperative to wrest the authority from the hands of those who had proved themselves incapable for good and who were fast losing all capability even for active harm. It was necessary to oppose our political method through the mobilization of all forces around the Soviets, through the All-Russian Congress of the Soviets, through a rising, to their method of action through an artificially selected " Provisional Parliament " and a problematic Constituent Assembly. This could only be accomplished by an open and public break with the body created by Tsereteli and his friends, and by concentrating all the attention and strength of the working class on the Soviet organizations. It was for these reasons that I proposed a demonstrative exit from the Democratic Conference and a revolutionary agitation in the factories and among the troops against the attempt to adulterate the will of the Revolution and again to direct its further course into the groove of co-operation with the bourgeoisie. Lenin expressed himself in the same sense in a letter which we received a few days later. But among the leaders of the party there was still considerable hesitation. The July days had left a very deep impression on the party. The masses of workers and soldiers had shaken off the impression made by the July reprisals much more rapidly than many of our leading comrades who feared the break-up of the Revolution by another premature attempt on the part of the masses. In our group at the Democratic Conference I obtained fifty votes for my proposal against seventy cast in favour of participating in the Democratic Council. But our experience on that Council very soon strengthened the left wing of the party. It became only too evident that the method of compromises bordering on mere swindles, which had for its aim to secure the leadership of the Revolution for the propertied classes assisted by the Coalitionists who had lost all footing amongst the wide masses, was not the way out of the impasse into which the flabby middle-class democrats had brought the Revolution. By the time when the Democratic Council, supplemented by representatives of the propertied classes, became transformed into a " Provisional Parliament," the psychological readiness of our party to break away from this body was already ripe.

THE SOCIALIST REVOLUTIONARIES AND THE MENSHEVIKS.

The question before us at the time was whether the Socialist Revolutionaries of the Left would follow us along this path. This group was then in the process of formation, which from our party point of view was much too slow and hesitating. At the beginning of the Revolution, the Socialist Revolutionary Party became by far the strongest in the whole political field. The peasants, soldiers, and even the masses of the workers voted for the Socialist Revolutionaries.

They themselves had not expected anything of the kind, and more than once it had seemed as though there was a danger that the party might choke in the waves of its own success. With the exception of the purely capitalist and land-owning classes and the well-to-do intellectuals, all and everybody flocked to the banners of the Socialist Revolutionaries. And this entirely corresponded to the first stage in the Revolution, when the class boundaries had not yet had time to make themselves visible, when the yearning after a united revolutionary front found expression in the nebulous programme of a party which was ready to shelter alike the workers afraid of losing contact with the peasantry, the peasants seeking land and freedom, the intellectuals anxious to guide both these classes, and the official trying to adapt himself to the new order of things. When Kerensky, who, under the Tsarist Government, had belonged to the " Group of Toil," joined the Socialist Revolutionaries after the victory of the Revolution, the popularity of this party began to grow in correspondence with the advance of Kerensky himself along the road of power. Many colonels and generals, out of respect—not always platonic—for the War Minister, hastened to inscribe their names in the rolls of the party of the erstwhile terrorists. The old Socialist Revolutionaries, belonging to the old revolutionary school, were already at that time regarding somewhat uneasily the ever-growing number of " March "

Socialist Revolutionaries, that is to say, those members who had only found their revolutionary souls in March, after the Revolution had overthrown the old regime and had raised the Socialist Revolutionaries to power. In this way the party contained in its amorphousness not only the internal contradictions of the developing Revolution, but also all the prejudices of the backward peasant masses and all the sentimentalism, instability, and ambitions of the intellectual sections of the population. It was quite evident that the party could not exist long in such a form. In point of ideas it proved to be impotent from the very beginning. It was the Mensheviks who played the leading political rôle in the first stages of the Revolution. They had passed through the Marxian school, and had derived from it certain methods and habits which had helped them to find their way sufficiently in the political situation to adulterate " scientifically " the real meaning of the present class struggle and to secure, in the highest degree possible under the given conditions, the supremacy of the Liberal bourgeoisie. This is the reason why the Mensheviks, who were the direct advocates of the right of the bourgeoisie to power, so quickly spent themselves and were, by the time of the November Revolution, finally reduced almost to a cipher.

The Socialist Revolutionaries were also losing their influence more and more, first among the workers, then in the army, and finally also in

THE RUSSIAN REVOLUTION

the villages.   Nevertheless, at the time of the
November Revolution they were still numerically
a very powerful party.   But class antagonisms
were undermining it from within.   As against
its right wing, which in the persons of its
most chauvinist elements, such as Avksentieff,
Breshko-Breshkovskaya, Savinkoff and others,
finally went over to the counter-revolutionaries,
a left wing was in process of formation, which
tried to maintain a contact with the labouring
masses.   If we bear in mind the fact that the
Socialist Revolutionary Avksentieff, in his
capacity as Minister of the Interior, was arresting
the peasant land committees consisting almost
entirely of Socialist Revolutionaries, for their
grappling with the agrarian question on their
own authority, the amplitude of disagreements
within this party will become sufficiently
clear.

In the centre stood the traditional leader of
the party, Tchernoff.   An experienced writer,
well read in Socialist literature, an old hand in
party struggles, he was the invariable leader of
the party at the time when the party's life concentrated in refugees' circles abroad.   The
Revolution, which, in its first indiscriminate
onward rush, had raised the Socialist Revolutionaries to a tremendous height, automatically
also raised Tchernoff, but only to show his complete incapability even among the leading political
personages of the first period.   Those minor
qualifications which secured for Tchernoff a pre-

ponderance in the foreign circles of the party proved to be far too light in the scales of the Revolution. He confined himself to abstaining from all responsible decisions, to avoiding and evading all critical issues, to waiting upon events, and to refraining from all positive activity. Such tactics secured to him, for the time being, the position of a centre between the two flanks of the party, the distance between which was growing ever wider and wider. But the unity of the party could no longer be maintained. Savinkoff, the erstwhile terrorist, had taken part in the Korniloff plot, was on most cordial terms with the counter-revolutionary circles of the Cossack officers, and was preparing a crushing blow for the Petrograd workers and soldiers, amongst whom were not a few Socialist Revolutionaries of the Left. As a sop to this left wing, the Centre expelled Savinkoff from the party, but it dared not raise its hand against Kerensky.

In the Provisional Parliament the party showed itself to be hopelessly divided. The three groups acted independently of one another, although all were marching under the same party banner. At the same time none of these groups had any clear idea as to what it wanted. The formal predominance of this party in the Constituent Assembly would only have meant the continuation of the same political sterility and impotence.

THE RUSSIAN REVOLUTION

THE VOICE OF THE FRONT.

Before leaving the Provisional Parliament, where, according to the political statistics of Kerensky and Tsereteli, we only had about fifty seats, we organized a meeting with the Left Socialist Revolutionary group. They, however, refused to follow us, on the ground that it was necessary for them to prove to the peasantry by a practical experiment the hopelessness of that Parliament. "We think it our duty to warn you," said one of their leaders, "that if you mean to leave the Provisional Parliament with the object of immediately descending into the street for an open struggle, we shall not follow you." The bourgeois and Coalitionist Press accused us of aiming at a break-up of the Provisional Parliament for the sole purpose of creating a revolutionary situation. Our group in the Provisional Parliament decided not to wait for the Left Socialist Revolutionaries, but to act independently. The declaration of our party, read from the rostrum of the Provisional Parliament and explaining our reason for breaking away from this institution, was met with a howl of execration and impotent rage from the majority groups. In the Petrograd Soviet, where our action was approved by an overwhelming majority, the leader of the small group of "Internationalist" Mensheviks, Martoff, argued with us that our exit from the Provisional Council of the Republic (such was the official designa-

65

tion of this disreputable institution) would only then have any sense if we intended to pass immediately to an open offensive against the present Government. But that was just what we did intend doing. The agents of the Liberal bourgeoisie were quite right when they accused us of desiring to create a revolutionary situation. We saw that the only way out of the hopeless state of affairs was by means of an open rising and a direct seizure of power.

Again, as during the July days, the Press and all other organs of so-called public opinion were set in motion against us. The most poisonous weapons were once more got out of the arsenals of the July days, where they had been deposited after the Korniloff rising. Vain efforts! The masses flocked to us irresistibly, and their spirit rose hourly higher and higher. Delegates would arrive from the trenches and ask us, at the sittings of the Petrograd Soviet: "How long will this unbearable situation last? The soldiers have authorized us to tell you that if by the 15th of November no decisive steps are taken towards peace, the trenches will be evacuated, and the whole army will march back to the rear!" Such a resolve had really spread all along the front. The soldiers were distributing from one sector to the other proclamations drawn up by themselves, calling on all soldiers not to remain in the trenches after the first snow. "You have forgotten all about us," the trench delegates would exclaim at the sittings of the Soviet; "if you do not find some way out, we shall come here ourselves and scatter our enemies with our bayonets, but you, too, together with them." Within a few weeks the Petrograd Soviet became the centre of attraction for the whole army. After the change of its policy and the new election of its Presidential Bureau, its resolutions had been infusing into the exhausted and despairing troops new hopes that a way out of the impossible situation might at length be found on the lines laid down by the Bolsheviks, namely, by the publication of the secret treaties and the immediate proposal of an armistice on all fronts. " You say that full authority should pass into the hands of the Soviets? Then take it. Are you afraid that the front may not support you? Cast aside all doubt.; the overwhelming mass of the soldiers are entirely on your side."

In the meantime the conflict regarding the evacuation of the Petrograd garrison was proceeding apace. There were almost daily meetings of the garrison, consisting of company, regimental, and other committees. The influence of our party in the garrison became absolute and quite undivided. The Staff of the Petrograd military district was in a state of extreme confusion. At one time they would try to enter into regular relations with us.; at other times, urged on by the leaders of the Central Executive Committee, they would threaten us with repression.

THE COMMISSIONERS OF THE MILITARY REVOLUTIONARY COMMITTEE.

We have already mentioned the formation of a special Military Revolutionary Committee attached to the Petrograd Soviet, which was intended by us as a sort of Soviet Staff of the Petrograd garrison, by way of a counter-weight to Kerensky's Staff. " But the existence of two Staffs cannot be tolerated," urged the doctrinaire representatives of the Coalitionist parties. " Is, however," we replied, " a state of things tolerable in which the garrison has no confidence in the official Staff and fears that the removal of troops from Petrograd may be dictated by some new counter-revolutionary design? " " But the creation of a new Staff means an insurrection," argued the Right; " your Military Revolutionary Committee will have for its aim not so much the examination of the military intentions and orders of the military authorities, as the preparation and execution of a revolt against the present Government." This argument was perfectly just, but for this very reason it did not frighten any of us. The necessity of overthrowing the Coalition Government was recognized by the overwhelming majority of the Soviet. The more convincingly the Mensheviks and Socialist Revolutionaries were demonstrating that the Military Revolutionary Committee would inevitably become an instrument of revolt, the more readily did the Petrograd Soviet support this new militant organ.

The first business of the Military Revolutionary Committee was to appoint Commissioners to all sections of the Petrograd garrison and to all the most important institutions of the capital and suburbs. We received intelligence from various quarters that the Government, or, rather, the Government parties, were busily organizing and arming their forces. From different stores, Government and private, they were removing rifles, revolvers, machine guns and cartridges for the purpose of arming the cadets, students, and, generally, the young bourgeoisie. It was essential to take some preventive measures at once. Commissioners were appointed to all stores and depots of arms, and they became masters of the situation practically without opposition. True, the commandants and proprietors of the stores tried to refuse them recognition, but it was suf-

soldiers' committee or to the employees of the particular store in order to break down the almost immediately. Henceforth arms

Commissioners.

The regiments of the Petrograd garrison, indeed, had had their Commissioners before this, but they used to be appointed by the Central Executive Committee. We have already mentioned that after the June Congress of the Soviets, partic   demon   ti   of

July 1st, which showed the growing strength
of the Bolsheviks, the Coalitionist parties had
almost entirely shut out the Petrograd Soviet from
all practical influence on the course of events
in the revolutionary capital. The direction of
the affairs of the Petrograd garrison was concentrated in the hands of the Central Executive
Committee. Now the question was how to install
Soviet Commissioners everywhere. This was only
accomplished thanks to the energetic co-operation
of the masses of the soldiers. Regiment after
regiment would declare, at the end of meetings
addressed by speakers from various parties, that
they would only recognize the Commissioners
appointed by the Petrograd Soviet, and would
do nothing without their sanction.

In the appointment of these Commissioners the
military organization of the Bolsheviks played
a very important part. Already before the July
days this organization had done a great deal of
propaganda work. On July 18th the cycling
battalion, brought into Petrograd by Kerensky,
had sacked the villa of Mlle. Krzeszinska, where
the military organization of our party was located.
The majority of its leaders and many of the rank
and file were arrested, the papers were suppressed,
and the printing machinery was destroyed. Only
very slowly did the party again set up its press,
but this time " underground." Its military
organization embraced only a few hundred men
of the Petrograd garrison, but they included many
determined and absolutely devoted revolutionary

soldiers, young officers, and, principally, ensigns who had been imprisoned by Kerensky during July and August. All these now placed themselves at the disposal of the Military Revolutionary Committee and were appointed to the most responsible militant posts.

It will not be out of place, however, to note here that it was exactly the members of the military organization of our party who, in November, adopted an attitude of extreme caution and even of some scepticism towards the idea of an immediate rising. The exclusive character of the organization and its avowedly military character involuntarily inclined its leaders to overestimate the importance of the purely technical means of an insurrection, and from this point of view we were undoubtedly very weak. Our strength lay in the revolutionary spirit of the masses and in their readiness to fight under our banner.

THE SWELLING TIDE.

Side by side with the work of organization a raging and tearing agitation was being carried on. It was a period of incessant meetings at factories, in the " Modern " and Ciniselli Circuses, in the clubs and barracks. The atmosphere at all these meetings was decidedly electric. Every mention of an insurrection was met with a storm of applause and cries of approval. The bourgeois Press only intensified the general state of alarm. My order to the

Sestroretski Small Arms Factory about the issue of 5,000 rifles to the Red Guard called forth an indescribable panic in bourgeois circles. They talked and wrote constantly about a general massacre that was being prepared. This, of course, did not in the least prevent the workers of the Sestroretski Factory from issuing arms to the Red Guards. The more furiously the bourgeois Press slandered and execrated us, the more ardently did the masses respond to our call. It became more and more evident to both sides that the crisis was bound to come to a head in the course of the next few days. The Socialist Revolutionary and Menshevik Press were frantically agitated: " The Revolution is in the greatest danger ! A repetition of the July days is being prepared on an immensely greater scale and will therefore be bound to have still more ruinous results."

Gorki, in his paper *Novaya Zhizn* (" New Life "), daily prophesied the coming collapse of the whole cultural life of the country. In general, the Socialist red paint was vanishing with astonishing rapidly from the bourgeois intellectuals as the stern reign of the working-class dictatorship drew nearer. On the other hand, the soldiers, even of the more backward regiments, were greeting the Commissioners of the Military Revolutionary Committee with enthusiasm. Delegates were arriving from Cossack troops and from the Socialist minority amongst the cadets, promising, in case of an open collision, to secure, at least, the neutrality of their men. It was evident that Kerensky's Government was simply hanging in the air, without any firm ground under its feet.

The Military Staff of the district entered into negotiations with us and proposed a compromise. In order to get an idea of the strength of resistance of our foe we entered into pourparlers. But the nerves of the Staff were all on edge. Now they would admonish, then they would threaten us, and even declared that our Commissioners were illegal—which ban, of course, did not in the least interfere with their work. The Central Executive Committee, in agreement with the Military Staff, appointed Staff Captain Malevsky to be Chief Commissioner for the Petrograd military district, and generously consented to recognize our Commissioners, provided they were subordinated to their Chief Commissioner. This proposal was rejected and the negotiations were broken off.

Prominent Mensheviks and Socialist Revolutionaries would come to us as mediators, reason with and threaten us, foretelling our doom and the doom of the Revolution.

THE PETROGRAD SOVIET DAY.

The building of the Smolny Institute was at that time already in the hands of the Petrograd Soviet and of our party. The Mensheviks and the Right Socialist Revolutionaries had moved to Marie Palace, where the scarcely born Provisional Parliament was almost breathing its last. Kerensky made a great speech in the Provisional Parliament, in which, accompanied by the stormy applause of the bourgeois section, he attempted to conceal his impotence behind hysterical threats. The Military Staff made a last attempt at resistance. It sent an invitation to various units of the garrison, asking them to appoint two delegates from each unit to discuss the question of the evacuation of troops from the capital. The conference was fixed for one o'clock, November 4th. The regiments immediately informed us of this invitation, and we at once called a meeting of the garrison over the telephone for eleven o'clock in the morning. Some of the delegates, however, found their way to the Staff, but only to declare that without the permission of the Petrograd Soviet they would not go an inch anywhere. The garrison meeting almost unanimously reaffirmed its loyalty to the Military Revolutionary Committee. Opposition came only from the official representatives of the former Soviet parties, but it found no support whatever among the delegates of the regiments. The attempt of the Military Staff only showed the more clearly that the ground beneath our feet was firm. In the front ranks stood the Volhynian Regiment—the same one which, on the night of July 16th-17th, had marched to the strains of its band into the Taurida Palace for the purpose of putting down the Bolsheviks.

The Central Executive Committee, as was

THE RUSSIAN REVOLUTION

stated above, held possession of the funds and the Press of the Petrograd Soviet. All efforts to obtain possession even of one of these papers had proved of no avail. Hence about the middle of October steps had been taken to establish an independent paper for the Petrograd Soviet. But all the printing establishments were occupied, and their owners boycotted us, with the connivance of the Central Executive Committee. It was, therefore, decided to organize a Petrograd Soviet Day for the purpose of promoting an extended propaganda and collecting money for the establishment of a paper. This day had been fixed a fortnight previously for November 4th, and thus coincided with the date when the insurrection was publicly coming to view. The hostile Press was announcing it as an established fact that in November there would be an armed rising of the Bolsheviks in the streets of Petrograd. No one doubted that there would be a revolt. The only question was when. Efforts were made to guess and to predict, in order to elicit from us either a denial or an admission. All in vain. The Soviet calmly and confidently was forging ahead, paying no heed to the howl of bourgeois public opinion.

November 4th became the day of the review of the forces of the proletarian army. It went off splendidly in all respects. In spite of the warnings emanating from the Right that rivers of blood would flow in the streets of Petrograd on that day, the masses of the people poured out

into the streets in huge waves to take part in
the meetings of the Soviet. All our oratorical
strength was made full use of.; all public places
were packed*; meetings went on continuously
for hours. These were addressed by speakers
from our party.; by delegates who had come
from different parts of the country to take part
in the Congress of Soviets.; by speakers from
the front, from the Left Socialist Revolutionaries, and from the Anarchists. The halls
were simply overwhelmed by the masses of
workers and soldiers. There had been few
such meetings in Petrograd even during the
Revolution.

A considerable section of the lower middle
class was greatly disturbed—not so much actually
frightened as made uneasy by the warnings and
slanders of the bourgeois Press. Tens of
thousands of people beat in huge waves against
the walls of the People's Palace, overflowed into
the corridors, and filled the halls. From the
columns enormous garlands of human heads,
hands, and feet were hanging down like bunches
of grapes. The air seemed impregnated with
an electric current, such as is felt at the most
critical moments of a revolution. " Down with
Kerensky's Government ! " " Down with the
war ! " " All authority to the Soviets ! " Not
one of the representatives of the former Soviet
parties dared step forward before this colossal
gathering with a word of opposition. The
triumph of the Petrograd Soviet was unique and

undivided. The campaign was in reality already won. All that remained was to deal the phantom Government a final military blow.

THE GAINING OVER OF THE WAVERING UNITS.

The more cautious elements in our own midst, however, warned us that there were still some units of troops which were not with us—the Cossacks, the Cavalry Regiment, the Semenoff Guards, and the Cyclist Regiment. Propagandists and Commissioners were appointed to these units. Their reports seemed perfectly satisfactory. The heated atmosphere was affecting every one and everything, and even the most conservative elements of the army were unable to withstand the general tendency of the Petrograd garrison.

I went to an open-air meeting of the Semenoff regiment which was considered to be the chief support of the Kerensky Government. The best-known speakers of the Right wing were there. They clung to the conservative regiment of the Guards as to the last prop of the Coalition Ministry. But it was of no avail. The regiment declared in our favour by an overwhelming majority, and did not even allow the former Ministers to finish their speeches. Those groups which still opposed the demands of the Soviet consisted mainly of officers, volunteers, and, generally, of the middle-class intellectuals and semi-intellectuals. The workers and peasant

masses were wholly on our side. The cleavage
was pretty well along a straight social line.

The central military basis of Petrograd is the
Peter and Paul Fortress. We appointed as its
commandant a young ensign who soon proved
himself to be almost born for the place and in
a few hours became complete master of the
situation. The "lawful" military authorities
stepped aside to wait and see what might
happen.

For reasons given above, the Cyclist Regiment
was considered by us a very unreliable unit.
On November 5th I went to the fortress at about
two o'clock in the afternoon. In the courtyard
a meeting was being held. The speakers of
the Right wing were most cautious and evasive,
carefully avoiding any question about Kerensky,
whose name, even in soldiers' circles, always
gave rise to cries of protest and indignation.
They, however, listened to us and adhered to
us. At four o'clock the cyclists held a battalion meeting in a neighbouring place, in the
Modern Circus. Amongst the speakers was
the Quartermaster-General Paradeloff. He, too,
spoke very, very cautiously. Far gone were the
days when the official and semi-official orators
never spoke of the workers' party otherwise than
as a band of traitors and hirelings of the
German Kaiser. The Assistant-Chief of the
Staff came up to me and said: "Let us, for
goodness' sake, come to some understanding."
But it was now too late. Against only thirty

votes, the battalion declared itself, after a debate, in favour of the assumption of authority by the Soviets.

THE BEGINNING OF THE INSURRECTION.

The Kerensky Government was casting about for help from one quarter to another. It recalled two new cyclist battalions from the front and a mortar battery, and tried to call out some cavalry. The cyclists, when on their way, sent a telegram to the Petrograd Soviet: " We are being taken to Petrograd. We do not know for what purpose. Kindly explain." We asked them to stop and to send a delegation to us. When the latter arrived, they declared at the meeting of the Soviet that the battalion was entirely on our side. This aroused a new storm of enthusiasm. The battalion was ordered to enter the town immediately.

The number of delegates from the front increased day by day. They came for information on the position of affairs. They took our literature and went back to the front in order to spread the news that the Petrograd Soviet was carrying on a struggle for the assumption of authority by the workers, soldiers, and peasants. " The trenches will support you," they told us. The old army committees, on the other hand, which had not been re-elected for the last four or five months, were sending us threatening telegrams. But these frightened no one. We knew perfectly well that the committees were quite out of touch with the masses of the soldiers, as was the Central Executive Committee in regard to the local Soviets.

The Military Revolutionary Committee appointed Commissioners to all the railway stations. They kept all in-coming and out-going trains under close observation, and particularly watched all movements of troops. A continuous telephonic and motor connection was set up with all neighbouring towns and their garrisons. It was the duty of all the Soviets in agreement with the Petrograd Soviet to see to it that no counter-revolutionary troops, or rather troops deceived by the Government, entered Petrograd. The lower ranks of the railway servants at the stations and railway workers gave ready recognition to our Commissioners.

On November 6th a difficulty arose at the Telephone Exchange. We were refused connection. The cadets had entrenched themselves at the Central Telephone Exchange, and under their protection the telephone girls came out in opposition to the Soviet. This was the first manifestation of the future *sabotage* of the officials and civil servants. The Military Revolutionary Committee sent a detachment to the Telephone Exchange and put two small guns at the entrance. So began the seizure of the administrative offices. Sailors and Red Guards were stationed in small detachments at the Telegraph Office, at the Post Office, and other public offices, and measures were taken to gain possession of the State Bank. The Soviet Centre, the Smolny Institute, was converted into a fortress. In the attic there we still had, as a legacy from the Central Executive Committee, a score or so of machine guns, but they had been neglected, and the men in charge of them had lost all discipline. We summoned to the Smolny an additional machine-gun detachment, and early in the morning the soldiers were loudly wheeling their machine guns along the long stone corridors of the Smolny Institute. Some Mensheviks and Socialist Revolutionaries, who were still at the Institute, would now and then put their heads out of the doors with astonished or frightened faces. The Soviet and also the garrison held daily meetings at the Institute.

On the third floor, in a small corner room, the Military Revolutionary Committee was in permanent session. Hither flowed all information regarding the movements of troops, the frame of mind of soldiers and workers, the progress of propaganda in the barracks, the doings of the hooligans, the conferences held by the bourgeois politicians, life in the Winter Palace, and the intentions of the former Soviet parties. Our informants came from every quarter, and included workers, officers, house porters, Socialist cadets, servants, and fashionable ladies. Many brought only ridiculous nonsense; others, however, gave us very valuable information. The decisive moment was drawing near. It was clear that there could be no turning back.

THE RUSSIAN REVOLUTION

On November 6th, in the evening, Kerensky came to the Provisional Parliament and demanded its approval of repressive measures against the Bolsheviks. But the Provisional Parliament was in a pitiful state of confusion and well-nigh dissolution. The Cadets were urging the Right Socialist Revolutionaries to accept a vote of confidence ; the Right Socialist Revolutionaries were exerting pressure on the Centre ; the Centre wavered; and the Left Socialist Revolutionaries were carrying on a policy of Parliamentary opposition. After a number of conferences, discussions and hesitations, the resolution of the Left wing was adopted, condemning the seditious movement of the Soviet, but placing the responsibility for this on the anti-democratic policy of the Government. At the same time, we were daily receiving by post letters informing us of the numberless death sentences passed on us, of infernal machines, of the imminent blowing up of the Smolny Institute, etc. The bourgeois Press was savage with hatred and fear. Gorki, completely forgetting his own " Song of the Falcon," continued to prophesy in his paper, the *Novaya Zhizn*, the coming end of the world.

The members of the Military Revolutionary Committee had not left the Smolny Institute for the last week. They slept in snatches on sofas, constantly wakened by couriers, scouts, cyclists, telegraphists, and telephone bells. The most anxious night was that of November 6th-7th. We were informed from Pavlovsk by telephone that the Government was summoning the artillerists from there and the ensigns from the Peterhoff School. Kerensky had collected in the Winter Palace cadets, officers, and " shockers." We ordered, by telephone, detachments of trustworthy military guards to bar all entrances to Petrograd and to send agitators to meet the detachments summoned by the Government. If they could not be kept back by reason, then arms were to be employed. All our conversations were carried on perfectly openly over the telephone, and were, therefore, accessible to the Government's agents.

Our Commissioners informed us that our friends were keeping watch over all entrances to Petrograd. A portion of the Oranienbaum cadets did, however, get past our barriers in the night, and we followed up their further movements by telephone. We strengthened the outside guards of the Smolny by summoning another company. We maintained a continuous connection with all parts of the garrison. Squads on duty kept watch in all regiments. Delegates from every unit were constantly, day and night, at the disposal of the Military Revolutionary Committee. An order was issued to put down ruthlessly every Black Hundred agitation, to use arms at the first attempts at street pogroms, and to act, if necessary, without mercy. During this decisive night all the most important points in the city passed into our hands almost without resistance, without fighting, without victims. The

State Bank was guarded by Government sentries and an armoured car. The building was surrounded from all sides by our detachments, the armoured car was seized unawares, and the Bank passed into the hands of the Military Revolutionary Committee without a single shot.

On the Neva, below the Franco-Russian Works, stood the cruiser *Aurora* undergoing repair. Her crew consisted entirely of sailors wholeheartedly devoted to the Revolution. When, at the end of August, Korniloff was threatening Petrograd, the sailors of the *Aurora* were summoned to protect the Winter Palace. And although they were already extremely hostile to Kerensky's Government, they knew that their duty was to repel the attempt of the counter-revolutionaries, and they took up their positions without a word. When the danger passed, they were again pushed aside. Now, in these days of the November insurrection, they were too dangerous. The Ministry of the Marine gave orders to the *Aurora* to get under way and leave Petrograd waters. The crew immediately informed us of this fact. We countermanded the order, and the cruiser remained ready, at any moment, to use all her forces on behalf of the Soviet authority.

THE DECISIVE DAY.

At the dawn of November 7th the men and women employed at the party's printing works came to the Smolny and informed us that the

THE RUSSIAN REVOLUTION

Government had stopped our chief party paper and also the new organ of the Petrograd Soviet. The printing works had had their doors sealed up by some Government agents. The Military Revolutionary Committee at once counter-manded the order, took both papers under its protection, and placed the high honour of pro-tecting the freedom of the Socialist Press from counter-revolutionary attempts on the valiant Volhynian Regiment. After this, work was resumed and went on continuously at the printing office, and both papers came out at the appointed hour.

The Government was still in session in the Winter Palace, but it had already become a mere shadow of its former self. It had ceased to exist politically. In the course of Novem-ber 7th the Winter Palace was gradually sur-rounded from all sides by our troops. At one o'clock in the afternoon, in the name of the Military Revolutionary Committee, I announced at the sitting of the Petrograd Soviet that Kerensky's Government no longer existed, and that, pending the decision of the All-Russian Congress of Soviets, the Government authority would be assumed by the Military Revolutionary Committee.

Lenin had left Finland some days pre-viously and was living in hiding in a working-class quarter in a suburb. On November 7th he came secretly to the Smolny. Judging by the newspapers, he had gained the impression that we were coming to a compromise with the Kerensky Government. The bourgeois Press had shrieked so much about the coming revolt, the march of armed soldiers in the streets, the pillage, and the inevitable rivers of blood, that it did not perceive the insurrection which, in reality, was now taking place, and accepted the negotiations between ourselves and the Military Staff at their face value. All this time, quietly, without any street fighting, without firing or bloodshed, one Government institution after another was being seized by highly disciplined detachments of soldiers, sailors, and Red Guards, in accordance with the exact telephone instructions emanating from the little room on the third floor of the Smolny Institute.

In the evening, the second All-Russian Congress of the Soviets held a preliminary meeting.

The report of the Central Executive Committee was submitted by Dan. He delivered an indictment against the rebels, the usurpers, and sedition-mongers, and tried to frighten the meeting by predicting the inevitable collapse of the insurrection, which in a day or two, he said, would be suppressed by troops from the front. His speech sounded exceedingly unconvincing and very much out of place in a hall in which the overwhelming majority of delegates were following with the greatest enthusiasm the victorious march of the Petrograd rising.

By this time the Winter Palace was surrounded, though not yet taken. From time to time shots were fired from the windows at the besiegers who were slowly and very carefully closing in upon the building. From the Peter and Paul Fortress a few shells were fired at the Palace, their distant sounds reaching the Smolny. Martoff, with impotent indignation, was speaking from the rostrum of civil war, and particularly of the siege of the Winter Palace where, among the other Ministers, there were— oh, horror of horrors !—members of the Menshevik Party. Two sailors, who had come to give news from the scenes of struggle, took the platform against him. They reminded our accusers of the July offensive, of the whole perfidious policy of the old Government, of the re-establishment of the death penalty for soldiers, of the arrests, of the sacking of revolutionary organizations, and vowed that they would either conquer or die. They it was who brought us the news of the first victims on our side on the Palace Square.

Every one rose as though moved by some invisible signal, and with a unanimity which is only provoked by a deep moral intensity of feeling sung a Funeral March. He who lived through this moment will never forget it. The meeting came to an abrupt end. It was impossible to sit there, calmly discussing the theoretical question as to the method of constructing the Government, with the echo reaching our ears of the fighting and firing at the walls of the Winter Palace, where, as a matter of fact, the fate of this very Government was already being decided.

The taking of the Palace, however, was a protracted business, and this caused some wavering amongst the less determined elements of the Congress. The Right wing, through its spokesmen, prophesied our early doom. All were waiting anxiously for news from the Winter Palace. After some time, Antonoff, who had been directing the operations, arrived. At once there was dead silence in the hall. The Winter Palace had been taken. Kerensky had taken flight. The other Ministers had been arrested and conveyed to the Peter and Paul Fortress. The first chapter of the November Revolution was at an end.

The Right Socialist Revolutionaries and the Mensheviks, numbering altogether about sixty persons, that is, about one-tenth of the Congress, left the meeting under protest. As they could do nothing else, they " threw the whole responsibility " for whatever might now happen on the Bolsheviks and the Left Socialist Revolutionaries. The latter were still wavering. Their past bound them closely to Tchernoff's party. The Right wing of this party had now shifted entirely towards the lower middle class and their intellectuals, to the well-to-do peasants in the villages; in all decisive questions it was marching hand in hand with the Liberal bourgeoisie against us. The more revolutionary elements of the party, reflecting the Radicalism of the social aspirations of the poorest peasantry, gravitated to the proletariat and its party. They were afraid, however, to cut the umbilical cord which bound them with the old party. When we were about to leave the Provisional Parliament, they refused to follow us and warned us against " adventures." But the insurrection forced them to choose either for or against the Soviet. Not without hesitation, they were concentrating their forces on the same side of the barricade where we stood.

THE FORMATION OF THE COUNCIL OF PEOPLE'S COMMISSIONERS.

The victory at Petrograd was complete. The Military Revolutionary Committee had the reins of power completely in its hands. We issued our first decrees abolishing the death penalty, ordering new elections to the army committees, and so on. But here we discovered that we were cut off from the provinces. The superior officials at the railways and in the post and telegraph administration were against us. The old army committees, the Town Councils, and Zemstvos continued to bombard the Smolny Institute with minatory telegrams, proclaiming war against us and promising to sweep away the rebels in a very short time. Our telegrams, decrees, and explanations could not reach the provinces, as the Petrograd Telegraph Agency refused to serve us. The capital being thus isolated from the rest of the country, there readily spread very perturbing and fantastic rumours.

THE RUSSIAN REVOLUTION

On perceiving that the Soviet had really assumed power, that the members of the old Government had been arrested, and that in the streets of Petrograd armed soldiers were masters of the situation, the bourgeois and Coalitionist Press raised a frenzied campaign against us, the like of which had never been known before. Scarcely a lie or calumny existed which they did not hurl against the Military Revolutionary Committee, its directors and Commissioners.

On November 8th a meeting of the Petrograd Soviet took place, at which were also present the delegates of the All-Russian Congress of the Soviets, the members of the garrison conference, and numerous members of the party. Here, for the first time after an interval of four months, Lenin and Zinovieff took the platform amidst a most enthusiastic ovation. But mixed with the joy of our victory was some uneasiness as to how the country would receive the news of the insurrection, and whether the Soviets would be able to maintain their power.

In the evening of the same day a meeting of the Congress of the Soviets took place, which was of prime importance. Lenin introduced two decrees, on peace and on the land. Both were adopted unanimously after a short discussion. At this meeting, too, a new central authority was formed—the Council of People's Commissioners.

The Central Committee of our party made an effort to come to an agreement with the Left

Socialist Revolutionaries. They were invited to take part in the formation of a Soviet Government. But they were undecided: they thought that the new Government ought to be formed from all the parties in the Soviet, on the basis of a coalition. The Mensheviks and the Right Socialist Revolutionaries, however, had broken off relations with the Congress of the Soviets, considering imperative a coalition with anti-Soviet parties. We could do nothing else than suggest that the Left Socialist Revolutionaries should endeavour to get their neighbours on the right to rejoin the revolutionary fold. And whilst they were busying themselves with this hopeless task, we considered ourselves bound to take the whole responsibility of government on our own shoulders. The list of People's Commissioners was consequently made up exclusively of Bolsheviks. There was undoubtedly a certain amount of political danger in this. The transformation was really a bit too sudden. Just to think of it: the leaders of this party had but yesterday lain under an accusation provided by Article 108 of the Code, that is to say, accused of high treason! But there was no other choice for us. The other Soviet groups hesitated and refused, preferring to wait upon events before committing themselves. And, after all, we had no doubt that our party alone was capable of producing a really revolutionary Government.

THE RUSSIAN REVOLUTION

THE FIRST DAYS OF THE NEW REGIME.

The decrees regarding land and peace, confirmed by the Soviet Congress, were printed in vast numbers of copies and distributed throughout the length and breadth of the country by delegates from the front, by peasant messengers coming from the villages, and by propagandists whom we sent to the provinces and trenches. At the same time we continued the organization and arming of the Red Guard, who, together with the old garrison and sailors, were performing the arduous guard duties. The Council of People's Commissioners was taking over one Government institution after another, but everywhere were meeting with the passive resistance of the higher and middle officials. The former Soviet parties did everything they could to get support from these classes and thus to organize a *sabotage* of the new authority. Our enemies were quite certain that the whole business was a mere episode, that it was only a question of a day or two, perhaps of a week, and the Soviet Government would be overthrown. . . . At the Smolny, the first foreign Consuls and members of the Embassies put in their appearance, impelled as much by business motives as by curiosity. Newspaper correspondents also hurried thither with their notebooks and cameras. All hastened to get a glimpse of the new Government, certain that in a day or two it would be too late.

90

THE RUSSIAN REVOLUTION

In the city complete order reigned. The sailors, soldiers, and Red Guards behaved in these first days with exemplary discipline and maintained stern revolutionary order.

Among our enemies there was a growing fear lest the " episode " should continue too long; and very soon they began to organize the first attack against the new Government. The initiative emanated from the Socialist Revolutionaries and Mensheviks. In the previous phases of the Revolution, they had not been anxious, and indeed had not dared, to take the entire power into their hands. In correspondence with their political position as go-betweens, they contented themselves with serving in the Coalition Government in the capacity of assistants, critics, friendly opponents, and apologists for the bourgeoisie. At all elections they conscientiously cast anathemas on the Liberal bourgeoisie, but in the Government they as regularly united with it. Thanks to these tactics, they succeeded in the course of the first six months of the Revolution in completely forfeiting the confidence of the popular masses and of the army, and now the November Revolution had finally hurled them from power. Yet only yesterday they had still considered themselves masters of the situation. The leaders of the Bolsheviks whom they persecuted had been obliged to live " illegally " and in hiding, just as under the Tsardom. To-day, however, the Bolsheviks were in power, and the former Ministers and the Coalitionists and their coadjutors were swept aside and left without any influence on the further course of events. They did not want and could not believe that this sudden transformation signified the beginning of a new epoch. They wanted and forced themselves to think that it was all a mere accident, a misunderstanding, which could be righted by a few energetic speeches and indicting articles, but at every turn they stumbled upon ever increasing and irresistible obstacles. Hence their blind and truly savage hatred towards us.

The bourgeois politicians would not, of course, make up their minds to go into the fire themselves. Instead, they were pushing forward the Socialist Revolutionaries and Mensheviks, who in their struggle against us had acquired all that energy which they had so sadly lacked when they were in semi-power. Their organs were spreading the most fantastic rumours and slanders. In their name appeared proclamations containing direct appeals to the people to destroy the new Government. They, too, organized the officials for *sabotage* and the cadets for military action against us. Throughout November 9th and 10th we continued to receive constant threats by telegram from the army committees, Town Councils, Zemstvos, and the managing committee of the railway union. The Nevsky Prospekt, the chief artery of the bourgeoisie of the capital, became more and more animated. The bourgeois youth were awakening from their torpor, and, urged on by the Press, were unfolding at the Nevsky Prospekt an energetic agitation against the Soviet Government. Helped by crowds of bourgeois cadets, they were disarming individual Red Guardsmen, and in side streets were shooting down sailors and Red Guards. A group of cadets seized the Telephone Exchange. They also made attempts to seize the Telegraph and Post Office. Finally, we were informed that three armoured cars had fallen into the hands of some unknown military organization hostile to us. The bourgeois elements were evidently raising their heads. The Press was announcing that we were fast approaching our last hour. Our people intercepted some secret orders from which it was clear that a military organization had been formed against the Petrograd Soviet at the head of which stood a so-called " Committee for the Defence of the Revolution " created by the City Council and the old Central Executive Committee. Both in the latter and in the City Council, the Right Socialist Revolutionaries and the Mensheviks were the leading parties. This Committee had at its disposal cadets, students, and many counter-revolutionary officers, who, behind the backs of the Coalitionists, were hoping to deliver a death-blow to the Soviets.

THE CADET RISING OF NOVEMBER 11TH.

The chief basis for the counter-revolutionary organizations was the Cadet and Engineering

Schools, where a considerable quantity of arms and munitions were stored and from which raids were carried out against the institutions of the Revolutionary Government.

Detachments of Red Guards and sailors surrounded the Cadet School and sent parlementaires to demand the surrender of arms. The besieged replied with bullets. The besiegers were marking time, and a crowd collected round them. Now and again a stray shot from within would hit a passer-by. The skirmish seemed to be getting prolonged indefinitely and was threatening to have a demoralizing effect on the revolutionary detachments. It was imperative to resort to drastic measures. The duty of disarming the cadets was then placed on the commander of the Peter and Paul Fortress, Ensign B——, who closely surrounded the Cadet School, brought up some armoured cars and artillery, and delivered an ultimatum to the cadets to surrender in ten minutes. They answered with renewed fire from the windows. At the end of the ten minutes, B—— commanded the artillery to open fire. The first shots made a wide gaping breach in the walls, and the cadets surrendered, although many of them tried to escape and, in so doing, continued firing at their pursuers. The exasperation and bitterness accompanying every civil war was soon engendered. The sailors undoubtedly committed cruelties on individual cadets. The bourgeois Press afterwards accused the sailors and the Soviet Government of inhumanity and savagery. But it was silent on one point : that the Revolution of November 7th-8th had been accomplished without a single shot and without a single victim, and that it was only the counter-revolutionary plot which had been organized by the bourgeoisie and which threw its young men into the cauldron of a civil war against the workers, soldiers, and sailors that led to inevitable atrocities and victims. The events of November 11th effected a radical change in the temper of the Petrograd people. The struggle took on a more tragic aspect. At the same time our enemies at length realized that the position of affairs was much more serious than they had thought, and that the Soviet by no means intended to give up the power it had just won, merely at the bidding of the capitalist Press and cadets.

The clearance of Petrograd of all counter-revolutionary hotbeds went on with great intensity. The cadets were disarmed almost entirely, and those who took part in the rising were arrested and imprisoned in the Peter and Paul Fortress, or taken to Kronstadt. Those papers which had been openly calling for a rising against the Soviet authority were suppressed. An order was also issued for the arrest of some of the leaders of the former Soviet parties whose names appeared in the intercepted counter-revolutionary correspondence. With this, all military resistance to the new authority was finally broken in the capital.

THE RUSSIAN REVOLUTION

Then followed a prolonged, and exhausting struggle with the " Italian " strike of officials, technical staffs, employees of Government departments, etc. These individuals, although belonging for the most part, in point of pay, to the oppressed class, adhere by their mode of life and their psychology to the bourgeoisie. They had faithfully served the State when Tsarism stood at its head, and they continued to serve it faithfully when authority passed into the hands of the Imperialist bourgeoisie. Afterwards, in the next period of the Revolution, they passed over with all their knowledge and their technical skill to the service of the Coalition Government. When, however, the insurgent workers, soldiers, and peasants hurled the exploiting classes from the helm of the State and tried to take the direction of affairs into their own hands, the officials and employees revolted and absolutely refused to support the new Government in any way whatever. As time went on, this *sabotage* spread more and more, its organizers being, in the main, Socialist Revolutionaries and Mensheviks, and its financial support being derived from the banks of the Entente Embassies.

KERENSKY'S ADVANCE ON PETROGRAD.

The growing stability of the Soviet's power in Petrograd made the middle-class groups transfer all their hopes to military help from outside. The Petrograd Telegraph Agency, the Railway Telegraph, and the Radio-Telegraph

Station of Tsarskoye Selo were sending wire after wire reporting that great military forces were moving on Petrograd with the object of suppressing the rebels and establishing order. Kerensky had fled to the front, and the papers of the bourgeois parties were announcing that he was leading numberless troops against the Bolsheviks. We were cut off from the rest of the country, as the telegraph stations refused to send our messages. But the soldiers who, by tens and hundreds, were daily coming to see us to bring messages from their regiments, divisions, and corps, all kept on saying to us: "Don't be afraid of the front; the whole front is entirely on your side ; give your orders and we are ready at a moment's notice to send a division or a corps to assist you." The army was in the same state as all the rest ; the rank and file were on our side, the upper ten against us. Of course, the upper ten had the technical military machinery in their hands. Various sections of our million-headed army found themselves isolated from one another. We, on our part, were isolated from the army and from the country. Nevertheless, the news of the Soviet's power at Petrograd and of its decrees was, in spite of all obstacles, spreading all over the country, and stirred the provincial Soviets to revolt against the old authority.

The news of Kerensky's march on Petrograd at the head of troops was soon confirmed and took a more definite shape. We were informed

G

from Tsarskoye Selo of the approach of Cossack échelons who had passed through Luga. A proclamation was distributed in the capital, signed by Kerensky and General Krasnoff, inviting the whole garrision to join the Government's troops who in a few hours' time would occupy Petrograd. The rebellion of the cadets on November 11th was undoubtedly connected with Kerensky's enterprise, but it burst out too soon, owing to our energetic action. An order was issued to the garrison of Tsarskoye Selo to call upon the advancing Cossacks' échelons to submit to the authority of the Soviet, and, in case of refusal, to disarm them. But the garrison of Tsarskoye Selo was ill-adapted for military operations. It had no artillery and no leaders, as the officers were hostile to the Soviet. The Cossacks seized the radio-telegraph station of Tsarskoye Selo, the most powerful of its kind in the country, and continued to advance. The garrisons of Peterhoff, Krasnoye Selo, and Gatchina showed no initiative and no resolution.

After an almost bloodless victory at Petrograd, the soldiers were convinced that, in future, things would continue the same course: it would be sufficient to send an able agitator to the Cossacks to explain to them the objects of the workers' revolution, and the Cossacks would lay down their arms. It was by means of speeches and fraternization that the Korniloff counter-revolutionary rebellion had been overpowered. It was by means of agitation and the cleverly planned seizure of offices that Kerensky's Government had been deposed without any fighting. The same methods were now being applied by the leaders of the Tsarskoye Selo, Krasnoye Selo, and Gatchina Soviets against the Cossacks of General Krasnoff, but this time without success. The Cossacks did not manifest any great enthusiasm or resolve, and continued to advance. Some of the Cossacks' detached sections reached Gatchina and Krasnoye Selo, a few skirmishes between them and the local garrisons took place, and some of the garrison troops were disarmed. We, at first, had no idea of the size of Kerensky's forces. Some asserted that General Krasnoff was at the head of ten thousand men, others estimated that he could not have more than one thousand, while the papers and manifestoes of the hostile parties were announcing in huge letters that two corps were concentrated near Tsarskoye Selo.

A state of uncertainty also reigned in the Petrograd garrison. Scarcely had they won one bloodless victory than they had to come out against an enemy, whose strength was unknown, and wage battles the issue of which was uncertain. The plan of sending fresh agitators and proclamations to the Cossacks was being constantly discussed at garrison conferences, since it seemed inconceivable to the soldiers that the Cossacks could refuse to adopt the standpoint which the Petrograd garrison had fought to assert. Meanwhile, the advance sections of the

Cossacks were approaching Petrograd, and we expected that the decisive struggle would take place in the streets of the capital.

The greatest determination was shown by the soldiers of the Red Guard. They demanded arms, munitions, and leaders. But the whole of the military machine was in a state of complete disorganization, partly from neglect and partly from malice. The officers had gone, many of them had fled; rifles were in one place, munitions in another. Our artillery was in a still worse condition. Guns, gun-carriages, shells were scattered here and there, and had to be searched for in all sorts of places. The regiments were short of engineering tools and field telephones. The revolutionary Staff, which tried hard to restore order from above, stumbled against insurmountable obstacles, chiefly in the shape of the *sabotage* organized by the military technical personnel.

We then decided to make a direct appeal to the working classes. We explained to them that all the conquests of the Revolution were at stake, and that only their energy, initiative, and self-sacrifice could save them and consolidate the new regime of the Workers and Peasants' Government. This appeal was crowned almost instantly with great practical success. Thousands of workmen came out and moved towards the positions occupied by Kerensky's troops and began to dig trenches. The workmen in the gun factories took in hand the fitting up of guns, the supply of munitions from the military stores, the requisition of horses ; they placed the guns in position, organized the commissariat department, obtained engines, motors, and cars, requisitioned the stocks of provisions and fodder, arranged sanitary columns—in a word, they built up and prepared for battle that military machine which we had in vain tried to create from above by the authority of the revolutionary General Staff.

When dozens of guns appeared in position, the spirit of our soldiers changed at once. Under cover of artillery they were ready to resist the attack of the Cossacks. The first line consisted of sailors and Red Guards. A few officers, whose political ideas were not ours, but who were honestly devoted to their regiments, led their soldiers to their positions and superintended their activities against Krasnoff's Cossacks.

THE COLLAPSE OF KERENSKY'S ADVENTURE.

Meantime the telegraph here and abroad was busy spreading news according to which the Bolsheviks' adventure was at an end. Kerensky had entered Petrograd, and order had been restored by his iron hand. At the same time, the bourgeois Press of Petrograd, comforted by the proximity of Kerensky's troops, was telling its readers about the complete demoralization of the Petrograd garrison, about the Cossacks' irresistible advance and their numerous artillery, and was predicting the coming doom of the Smolny. Our greatest difficulty, as already stated, consisted in the absence of an efficient technical apparatus and of men able to direct the military activities. Even those officers who had conscientiously accompanied their soldiers to the positions declined to accept the post of Commander-in-Chief.

After various attempts to solve the problem we selected the following combination: a garrison meeting elected a committee of five persons who were charged with supreme control over all operations against the counter-revolutionary troops advancing on Petrograd. This committee then came to an agreement with the Colonel of the General Staff, Muravieff, who during Kerensky's regime had been in opposition, and now, on his own initiative, had offered his services to the Soviet Government.

On November 12th, in the night which was very cold, Muravieff and I motored to the military positions. Carts loaded with provisions, fodder, guns, and munitions, were moving all along the road in the same direction. All that had been organized by the workers of various factories. Pickets of Red Guards stopped our car several times in order to verify our pass. Since the first days of the November Revolution all the cars of the city had been commandeered, and without a pass from Smolny no car was allowed to move in the streets or suburbs of the capital. The vigilance of the Red Guard was beyond all praise. Armed with rifles, they had been standing round the small bonfires for hours and hours, and the sight of these young armed workmen standing in the snow in the light 'of bonfires was the best symbol of the proletariat Revolution.

We found a good number of guns at the positions, and there was no lack of munitions. The decisive action took place on that very day, between Krasnoye Selo and Tsarskoye Selo. After a fierce artillery bombardment, the Cossacks, who had advanced as long as they met with no serious resistance, hastily fell back. They had all along been misled by tales about the atrocities of the Bolsheviks who intended to sell Russia to the Kaiser. They had been made to believe that the whole garrison of Petrograd was impatiently expecting them as liberators. The first serious resistance made havoc in their lines and doomed the whole of Kerensky's adventure.

The retreat of General Krasnoff's Cossacks gave us a chance of retaking the radio station of Tsarskoye Selo, and I at once wired the news of the victory over Kerensky's troops.[1]

[1] Here is the text of the wire :—

PULKOVO VILLAGE STAFF, 2.10 a.m.

The night of November 12th–13th will become historical. The attempt of Kerensky to lead counter-revolutionary troops against the capital, the seat of the Revolution, has met with a decisive repulse. Kerensky is in retreat ;

103

THE RUSSIAN REVOLUTION

We subsequently learnt from our friends abroad that the German wireless stations had received an order from the High Command not to intercept this message. Thus the first action of the German Government, in respect of the November

we are advancing. Soldiers, sailors, and workmen of Petrograd have shown that they are anxious to, and know how to, assert the will and power of the workers' democracy with their arms. The bourgeoisie strove to isolate the revolutionary army; Kerensky attempted to crush it under the Cossack's heel. Both attempts have proved a miserable failure.

The great idea of the supreme power of the workers and peasants' democracy has consolidated the ranks of our army and steeled its will. The whole country will now perceive that the power of the Soviets is not a passing event, but an irrefutable fact of the rule of workers, soldiers, and peasants. The repulse of Kerensky is a repulse of the bourgeoisie, the landlords, and the Kornilovites. The repulse of Kerensky is the establishment of the people's right to a peaceful and free life, to land, bread, and power. The Pulkovo detachment has, by its valiant deeds, consolidated the cause of the Workers and Peasants' Revolution. A return to the past is impossible. There are still struggle, obstacles, and sacrifices in front of us. But the road is open and victory is certain.

Revolutionary Russia and the Soviet Government have a right to be proud of their Pulkovo detachment and its Commander, Colonel Walden.

Eternal memory to the fallen! Glory to the warriors of the Revolution, soldiers and officers faithful to the people!

Long live revolutionary, popular, Socialist Russia!

On behalf of the Council of the People's Commissioners,

L. TROTSKY.

November 13, 1917.

104

THE RUSSIAN REVOLUTION

events, betrayed the fear lest they should cause a fermentation in Germany itself. Austria-Hungary intercepted a portion of our message, and, as far as we know, it became the source of information from which all Europe learned that Kerensky's luckless attempt to regain power had ended in a miserable failure. Signs of fermentation were now apparent among Krasnoff's Cossacks. They began sending scouts to Petrograd and even official delegates to the Smolny. There they were able to see for themselves that perfect order reigned at Petrograd, maintained by the garrison which was supporting the Soviet Government. The disorganization among the Cossacks became the greater as they soon realized the absurdity of the idea of capturing Petrograd by means of a thousand or so cavalrymen, since the promised support from the front was not forthcoming.

Krasnoff, with his Cossacks, retreated towards Gatchina, and when we reached there the following day, the members of his staff were already practically prisoners in the hands of the Cossacks themselves. Our garrison at Gatchina was in occupation of all the most important positions. The Cossacks, although not disarmed, were absolutely incapable of further resistance. They desired one thing only, viz. to be allowed to return to the Don as soon as possible, or at least to the front.

The Gatchina Palace was a curious sight. All the entrances were guarded by strong pickets.

THE RUSSIAN REVOLUTION

At the gates were artillery and armoured cars. The spacious rooms of the Palace, the walls of which were covered with valuable paintings, were crowded with soldiers and sailors and Red Guardsmen. On the tables of costly wood were scattered soldiers' clothes, pipes, and sardine boxes. One of the rooms was occupied by the staff of General Krasnoff. The floor was covered with mattresses, soldiers' coats, and caps. The representative of the Military Revolutionary Committee who accompanied me entered the room occupied by the staff, lowered his rifle upside down with a clang, and, leaning on it, declared: "General Krasnoff, you and your staff are prisoners of the Soviet." Armed Red Guardsmen immediately took up posts at both doors of the room. Kerensky was not there; he had fled, as he fled previously from the Winter Palace. General Krasnoff described the circumstances of his escape in his written evidence handed in on November 14th. I publish here this curious document verbatim:—

November 14, 1917, 6 p.m.

It was about 3 p.m. when I was summoned by the Commander-in-Chief [Kerensky]. He was very agitated and nervous.

"General," said he, "you have betrayed me: your own Cossacks here definitely say that they will arrest me and hand me over to the sailors."

"Yes," said I, "they talk a good deal about

it, and I know that there is no sympathy with you anywhere."

" Do the officers say the same? "

" Yes; the officers are exactly those who are the most discontented with you."

" What shall I do? I shall have to take my life."

" If you are an honest man you will go at once with a white flag to Petrograd and appear before the Revolutionary Committee and talk the matter over as the head of the Government."

" Yes, I will do that, General ! "

" I will give you a guard and I will get a sailor to go with you."

" No ; any one but a sailor. You know Dybenko is here."

" I do not know who Dybenko is."

" He is my enemy."

" Well, nothing is to be done. You have engaged in a big game and you must take risks."

" Very well ; I will go to-night."

" Why in the night? That would be a flight. Go openly and calmly; let everybody see that you are not trying to escape."

" Very well. Only give me a convoy which I can trust."

" Agreed."

I went out, called a Cossack of the 10th Don Cossacks' Regiment, Russkoff, and ordered him to appoint eight Cossacks to form a bodyguard for the Commander-in-Chief.

Half an hour later the Cossacks came in to
tell me that they could not find Kerensky anywhere—that he had fled. I raised the alarm and
ordered a search to be made for him; I am
inclined to think that he could not have fled
from Gatchina and is still hiding somewhere
here.

MAJOR-GENERAL KRASNOFF,
Commander of the 11th Corps.

Such was the end of this business.

Nevertheless, our opponents did not want to
surrender or to admit that the question of government authority had been settled. They still
nourished hopes of help from the front. The
leaders of the ex-Soviet parties—Tchernoff,
Tsereteli, Avksentieff, Gotz, and others, one
after another, went to the front to negotiate with
the old army committees gathered at Dukhonin's
headquarters, tried to incite him to resist, and,
according to the Press, even attempted to form
at his quarters a new Ministry. But nothing
came of it. The old army committees had lost
all their influence, and the front was feverishly
busy calling together conferences for the new
elections to all the army organizations at the
front. At these re-elections the Soviets' regime
was everywhere victorious.

Meanwhile our detachments were moving by
rail further from Gatchina towards Luga and
Pskoff. There they met several trains with
" shockers " and Cossacks, who had either been

summoned by Kerensky or despatched by various generals. An armed conflict occurred between our troops and one of these Cossack échelons. But the majority of the soldiers sent from the front to Petrograd, on meeting with the representatives of the Soviet troops, immediately declared that they had been deceived and that they would not raise their arms against the authority of the workers and soldiers.

INTERNAL FRICTIONS.

In the meantime the struggle for the establishment of the Soviet regime was spreading all over the country. In Moscow this struggle was particularly protracted and bloody. Perhaps this was due not the least to the fact that the leaders of the Revolution did not act at once with all the determination needed in offensive operations. In a civil war, more than in any other, victory can be secured only by a prompt and continuous offensive. Hesitation is dangerous, negotiations are risky, the policy of marking time is ruinous. One must always remember that the masses of the people have never been in possession of power, that they have always been under the heel of other classes, and that therefore they lack political self-confidence. Any hesitation shown in the revolutionary centres has an immediate deteriorating effect on them. Only when the revolutionary party firmly and unflinchingly speeds to its goal can it help the working masses to overcome all the slavish instincts inherited from centuries and lead the masses to victory. Only a resolute offensive secures victory with a minimum expenditure of strength and with the least losses.

But the attainment of resolute and firm tactics is just the difficulty. The lack of confidence of the masses in their own strength, the lack of experience of power, are reflected also in the leaders who, besides, are all the time under the powerful pressure of bourgeois public opinion.

The bare idea of the possibility of the establishment of a Workers' Government filled our bourgeois Liberals with hatred and spite. These feelings they expressed in the numberless papers they had at their disposal. Next came our "intellectuals," who, with all their profession of Radicalism and the socialistic colouring of their thought, were yet harbouring in the depth of their consciousness a most slavish admission of the bourgeoisie's might and its art of ruling. All these intellectuals, with their socialistic plumage, at once shifted towards the Right, regarding the consolidation of the power of the Soviets as the beginning of the end. Following on the heels of the representatives of Liberal professions walked the old bureaucracy, the administrative and technical personnel, all those elements who, morally and materially, live on the crumbs falling from the table of the bourgeoisie. The opposition of all these classes was mostly of a passive character, especially after the suppression of the cadet rebellion, but for that very reason it often seemed insurmountable. At every step we were refused assistance. The officials would either leave the Government offices or, remaining there, refused point-blank to work for us. They would not surrender the books or funds. The telephone exchanges refused to connect us. The telegraph offices would mutilate or delay our messages. We could not find translators, stenographers, or even copyists, etc. All that created such an atmosphere that some among us, even some of those at the head of our party, began to doubt whether the working masses would be able, in face of such resistance on the part of the bourgeois classes, to set in order the machinery of Government and remain in power. Here and there were heard voices advising an agreement. But with whom? With the bourgeois Liberals? Such a coalition had been already tried, and it drove the Revolution into a terrible bog. The insurrection of November 7th was an act of self-preservation on the part of the masses, after a period of impotence and treason on the part of the Coalition Government. The only coalition which still remained to be tried was the coalition within the ranks of the so-called revolutionary democracy, that is, of all Soviet parties. Such a coalition we had virtually proposed from the very beginning, at the sitting of the second All-Russian Congress on November 7th. The Kerensky Government had just been overturned and we had proposed to the Soviet Congress to take over the government authority. But the parties of the Right had left us and banged the door behind them. And it was the very best they could have done. They represented but an insignificant section at the Congress. They were no longer supported by the masses, since even those sections of the people who, by their apathy, were still supporting them, were gradually drifting over to our side. The coalition with the Right wing of the Socialist Revolutionaries and Mensheviks would not have broadened the social basis of the Soviet Government.; at the same time it would have introduced into its personnel elements demoralized through and through by political scepticism and by worship of bourgeois Liberalism. All the strength of the new authority lay in the radicalism of its programme, in the determination with which it acted. To tie oneself to the groups of Tchernoff and Tsereteli would have meant to put shackles on the arms and legs of the new authority and to cause the masses to lose confidence in it in no time.

Our nearest neighbours on the right were the so-called " Left " Socialist Revolutionaries. On the whole they were quite ready to support us, but at the same time they desired to form a Coalition Socialist Government. The Central Committee of the Railway Union, the Central Committee of the Post and Telegraph Employees, the Union of Government Officials—all these organizations were against us. At the head of our own party some were-urging the need of coming to an agreement with these organizations in some way or other. But on what basis? All those above-mentioned leading organizations of the past regime had already outlived themselves. Their relationship to the lower officials was roughly the same as that of the old army committees to the soldier masses in the trenches. History had drawn a deep line of demarcation between the higher and lower strata. An un-principled alliance with these worn-out leading organizations of yesterday was doomed to an inevitable collapse. In order to overpower the *sabotage* and the aristocratic pretensions of those above, it was necessary to lean for support firmly and resolutely on the rank and file. We left to the Socialist Revolutionaries the task of continuing the hopeless attempts to effect a com-promise. Our own policy was, on the contrary, to mobilize those who laboured at the bottom of the scale against all those representative bodies which had supported the Kerensky regime. This uncompromising policy caused friction and even a split amongst the leaders of our own party. At the Central Executive Committee, the Left Socialist Revolutionaries protested against the severity of the measures adopted by the new Government, and insisted on the necessity of compromises. The protest was supported by a section of the Bolsheviks, and three People's Commissioners resigned and left the Govern-ment. Some other active members of the party expressed their fundamental solidarity with those who had resigned. This made a tremendous impression in various bourgeois and intellectual circles: it was now evident that the Bolsheviks, whom the cadets and the Cossacks of General Krasnoff had failed to crush, were bound to perish, together with the Soviet regime, as a result of internal dissolution. However, the masses never noticed the split at all, and unanimously supported the Council of the People's Commissioners not only against the counter-revolutionary plotters and the *saboteurs*, but also against all compromise-mongers and sceptics.

THE FATE OF THE CONSTITUENT ASSEMBLY.

When, after Korniloff's adventure, the paramount parties on the Soviets made an attempt to make amends for their previous attitude of indulgence towards the counter-revolutionary bourgeoisie, they demanded the speedy convocation of the Constituent Assembly. Kerensky, who had just been saved by the Soviets from the too close embrace of his ally Korniloff, was obliged to give in. The Constituent Assembly was fixed for the end of November. But the circumstances had by that time become such that no guarantee whatsoever was available that the Constituent Assembly would, indeed, be called together. Complete disorganization reigned at the front, the number of deserters was growing every day, and the soldiers threatened to leave the trenches in regiments and corps and to withdraw to the rear, devastating everything on their way. In the country districts seizures of private lands and live stock were going on in a most haphazard fashion. Martial law was in consequence proclaimed in many places. Meanwhile the German troops continued to advance, took Riga and threatened Petrograd. The Right wing of the bourgeoisie was openly rejoicing over the danger threatening the revolutionary capital. The Government offices had been evacuated from Petrograd, and Kerensky intended to transfer the seat of his Government to Moscow. All that made the possibility of the Constituent Assembly being called together not only remote, but well-nigh unlikely. From this point of view the November *coup d'état* may have been regarded as the salvation of the Constituent Assembly as well as of the Revolution as a whole. And when we argued that the road to the Constituent Assembly lay not through Tsereteli's Provisional Parliament, but through the seizure of power by the Soviets, we were absolutely sincere. But the endless postponements of the summoning of the Constituent Assembly had not been without effect on it. Announced in the first days of the Revolution, it made its appearance after eight or nine months of a severe struggle between classes and parties. It came too late to have still a chance of playing a constructive rôle. Its intrinsic futility had been predetermined by one single fact which at first might have appeared as of small importance, but which later on affected the fate of the Constituent Assembly tremendously.

During the first phases of the Revolution the party of the Socialist Revolutionaries had been numerically the strongest. I have already mentioned its amorphous condition and its mixed social composition. The Revolution had been irresistibly leading to the internal differentiation among those who were marching under the " Populist " banner. The left wing of this party, representing a portion of the industrial workers and the great masses of the poorer peasantry, was separating more and more from the rest, and ultimately found itself in an irreconcilable opposition to the leaders of the Socialist Revolutionary Party, who represented the lower and middle bourgeoisie. But the inertia of the party frame and traditions delayed the inevitable split. The proportional system of elections rests, as is well known, entirely on party lists. As these lists had been drawn up two or three months before the November Revolution, the names of the Left and the Right Socialist Revolutionaries figured *pêle-mêle* in the same list, under the banner of the same party. In this way, by the time of the November Revolution, when the Right Socialist Revolutionaries were already arresting members of the Left Socialist Revolutionaries, and the Left were joining the Bolsheviks for the overthrow of the Government of the Socialist Revolutionary Kerensky, the old lists were still retaining their validity, and peasants at the elections for the Constituent Assembly were obliged to vote for lists headed by Kerensky's name and containing names of Left Socialist· Revolution- aries who were taking part in the conspiracy against him.

The months preceding the November Revolu- tion were marked by an incessant orientation of the masses towards the Left and a wholesale flow of the workers, soldiers, and peasants into the ranks of the Bolsheviks. During the same period the same process was manifesting itself in the ranks of the Socialist Revolutionary Party in the shape of the extension of the Left wing at the expense of the Right. Yet three-fourths of the names figuring on the party lists of the Socialist Revolutionaries were those of the old leaders of the Right wing, whose revolutionary reputation had been forfeited completely during their coalition with the Liberal bourgeoisie.

To this must be added the fact that the elections took place during the first weeks follow- ing the November Revolution. The news of the change was spreading in slowly widening circles from the capital to the provinces, from the towns to the villages. In many places the masses of peasantry had a very vague idea of what had taken place in Petrograd and Moscow. They nominally voted for " Land and Liberty," for their representatives on the land committees, who, for the most part, were following the " Populist " banner. In effect, they were voting for Keren- sky and Avksentieff, who were dissolving those very land committees and arresting their members. The result of it all was a most incredible political paradox: one of the two parties which were to dissolve the Constituent Assembly, viz. the Left Socialist Revolutionaries, was actually elected on the same lists as the party which had obtained the majority in the Constituent Assembly. These facts show clearly what a belated product the Constituent Assembly was in comparison with the actual progress of party warfare and party differentiations. We must now examine the question also from the point of view of principle.

THE PRINCIPLES OF DEMOCRACY AND THE DICTATORSHIP OF THE PROLETARIAT.

As Marxists, we have never been worshippers of formal democracy. In a society split into classes, the democratic institutions, far from abolishing the class struggle, only lend the class interests a highly imperfect form of expression. The possessing classes have always at their disposal thousands of means to pervert and adulterate the will of the labouring masses. In time of revolution democratic institutions form a still less perfect apparatus for the expression of the class struggle. Marx called Revolution "the locomotive of history." The open and direct struggle for power enables the labouring masses to acquire in a short time a wealth of political experience and thus rapidly to pass from one stage to another in the process of their mental evolution. The ponderous mechanism of democratic institutions cannot keep pace with this evolution—and this in proportion to the vastness of the country and the imperfection of the technical apparatus at its disposal.

The Right Socialist Revolutionaries were in a majority at the Constituent Assembly. In accordance with parliamentary usage, they should have formed the Government. But the Right Socialist Revolutionaries had had the chance of forming such a Government during the whole period of Revolution before November. Yet they had refrained from doing so, had handed over the lion's share of power to the Liberal bourgeoisie, and exactly for that reason they had lost the last vestige of influence among the most revolutionary sections of the people by the very time when the numerical composition of the Constituent Assembly placed them under the formal obligation to assume the reins of government. The working class, together with the Red Guard, were deeply hostile to the Right Socialist Revolutionaries. The overwhelming majority of the army supported the Bolsheviks. The revolutionary elements in the villages divided their sympathies between the Left Socialist Revolutionaries and the Bolsheviks. The sailors, who had been so prominent in all the incidents of the Revolution, were almost to a man with our party. The Right Socialist Revolutionaries had, in fact, been compelled to leave the Soviets, which had assumed power in

November, that is, before the Constituent Assembly. On what support could a Ministry formed by such a majority of the Constituent Assembly depend? It would have had behind it the rich of the villages, intellectuals, and the old officialdom, and perhaps would have found support, for the time being, among the middle class. But such a Government would have been completely deprived of the material apparatus of power. In the centres of political life, like Petrograd, it would have met at once with an uncompromising resistance. If the Soviets had, in accordance with the formal logic of democratic institutions, handed over their power to the party of Kerensky and Tchernoff, the new Government, discredited and impotent, would have only succeeded in temporarily confusing the political life of the country, and would have been overthrown by a new rising within a few weeks. The Soviets decided to reduce this belated historical experiment to a minimum, and dissolved the Constituent Assembly on the very day when it assembled.

On this account our party has been made the butt of most violent accusations. No doubt the dissolution of the Constituent Assembly made a very unfavourable impression in the leading quarters of the Socialist parties of the West, and the politically unavoidable and necessary act was denounced there as a piece of party tyranny and sectarian arbitrariness. Kautsky, with his customary pedantry, explained in a series of articles the mutual relationship between the

THE RUSSIAN REVOLUTION

Socialist and Revolutionary tasks of the proletariat and the regime of political democracy.
He endeavoured to prove that the observance
of the principle of democracy was always, in the
last resort, advantageous to the working class.
Of course, in a general way, and on the whole,
that is true. But Kautsky reduced this historical
truth to a piece of professorial banality. If
it always, in the end, pays the proletariat to wage
its class struggle and even to exercise its dictatorship within the frame of democratic institutions,
it does not at all follow that history always
affords the chance of such a combination. It
does not follow from the Marxian theory at all
that history invariably creates conditions which
are the most " advantageous " to the proletariat.
It is at present difficult to say what course the
Revolution would have taken if the Constituent
Assembly had been summoned in its second or
third month. Very probably the parties of the
Socialist Revolutionaries and Mensheviks, which
then predominated, would have discredited themselves, together with the Constituent Assembly,
in the eyes not only of the more active elements
which were supporting the Soviets, but even in
those of the backward popular masses, whose
hopes would have been bound up, not with the
Soviets, but with the Constituent Assembly. In
such circumstances the dissolution of the Constituent Assembly might have been followed by
new elections from which the parties of the Left
would have emerged in a majority. But the

course of events went in a different direction. The elections to the Constituent Assembly took place in the ninth month of the Revolution, and by that time the class struggle had reached such a degree of intensity that it burst, by its internal pressure, the formal framework of democracy.

The proletariat led the army and lower masses of peasantry. These classes were in a state of direct and fierce revolt against the Right Socialist Revolutionaries. Yet, thanks to the cumbrous machinery of democratic elections, this party obtained a majority in the Constituent Assembly, representing the pre-November phase of the Revolution. This was a contradiction which could not be solved within the framework of formal democracy, and only political pedants, who do not clearly realize the revolutionary logic of the relations of classes, can, in face of the situation resulting from the November events, preach to the proletariat banal truths concerning the advantages of democracy for waging the class war.

History chose to put the problem in a form much more concrete and acute. The Constituent Assembly, by its composition, was obliged to hand over the reins of power to the Tchernoff-Kerensky-Tsereteli group. Was this group capable of guiding the Revolution? Could they find support in the class which formed the backbone of the Revolution? No. The material class-contents of the Revolution came into an irreconcilable conflict with its democratic forms. Thereby the fate of the Constituent Assembly was decided in advance. Its dissolution appeared as the only conceivable surgical way out of the contradictory situation which was not of our making, but had been brought about by the preceding course of events.

THE PEACE NEGOTIATIONS.

At an historical night sitting, the Second All-Russian Congress of Soviets adopted the historical Peace Decree. At that time the power of the Soviets was still only consolidating in the most important centres of the country, while the number of people abroad who had confidence in it was quite insignificant. We carried the decrees unanimously, but to many it appeared to be merely a political demonstration. The compromise-mongers kept repeating at every street corner that our resolution could not lead to any practical results, since, on the one hand, the German Imperialists would not recognize and would not even condescend to talk with us, and, on the other hand, our allies would declare war on us for entering into separate peace negotiations. It was under the shadow of these gloomy predictions that we were making our first steps towards a universal democratic peace. The Decree was accepted on November 8th, when Kerensky and Krasnoff were at the very gates of Petrograd, and on November 20th we communicated over the wireless our proposals for the conclusion of a general peace both to

our allies and enemies. By way of reply the
Allied Governments addressed, through their military agents, remonstrances to General Dukhonin,
the Commander-in-Chief, stating that all further
steps on our part towards separate peace negotiations would lead to most serious results. We,
on our part, replied on November 24th to this
protest by a manifesto to all workers, soldiers,
and peasants, declaring that under no circumstances should we allow our army to shed its
blood by order of any foreign bourgeoisie. We
brushed aside the threats of the Western Imperialists and assumed full responsibility for our
peace policy before the international working
class. First of all, by way of discharging our
previous pledges, we published the secret treaties
and declared that we repudiated all that was
opposed in them to the interests of the popular
masses everywhere. The capitalist Governments
tried to play off our disclosures against one
another, but the popular masses everywhere
understood us and appreciated our action. Not
a single Socialist patriotic paper, as far as we
know, dared protest against this radical change
effected by the Government of workers and
peasants in all traditional methods of diplomacy,
against our repudiation of its evil and unscru-
pulous intrigues. We made it the aim and purpose of our diplomacy to enlighten the popular
masses, to open their eyes as to the nature of
the policy of their respective Governments, and
to fuse them in one common struggle against, and

hatred of, the bourgeois-capitalist regime. The German bourgeois Press accused us of protracting the negotiations, but the peoples themselves eagerly listened everywhere to the dialogues at Brest, and thereby, in the course of the two and a half months during which the peace negotiations proceeded, a service was rendered to the cause of peace which has been acknowledged even by honest enemies. For the first time the question of peace was raised in such a way that it could no longer be distorted by any machinations behind the scenes.

On December 5th we signed the agreement for the suspension of hostilities along the whole front, from the Baltic to the Black Sea. We again appealed to the Allies to join us and to conduct the peace negotiations together with us. We received no answer, although this time our allies did not try to intimidate us by threats. The peace negotiations began on December 22nd, six weeks after the adoption of the Peace Decree. This shows that the accusations levelled at us by the hireling and Socialist traitor Press, that we had not tried to come to an understanding with the Allies, were nothing but lies. For six weeks we kept on informing them of every step we made, and constantly appealed to them to join us in the peace negotiations. We can face the people of France, Italy, and Great Britain with a clear conscience. We did all we could to prevail upon the belligerent nations to join us in the peace negotiations. The responsibility for our separate peace negotiations rests not upon us, but upon the Imperialists of the West, as well as those Russian parties which all along had been predicting an early death to the Workers and Peasants' Government and urging the Allies not to take seriously our peace initiative.

Anyhow, on December 22nd the peace negotiations were opened. Our delegates made a declaration of principles defining the basis of a general democratic peace in the precise terms of the Decree of November 8th. The other side demanded an adjournment of the sittings ; but their resumption was put off, on Kühlmann's motion, from day to day. It was obvious that the delegates of the Quadruple Alliance had considerable difficulty in drawing up their reply to our declaration. At last, on December 25th, the reply came. The diplomats of the Quadruple Alliance adhered to the democratic formulæ of a peace without annexations and contributions on the principle of self-determination of nations. We could see clearly that this was merely a piece of make-believe. But we did not expect even that, for is not hypocrisy the tribute paid by vice to virtue ? The fact that the German Imperialists considered it necessary to pay this tribute to our democratic principles was, in our eyes, evidence of the rather serious internal condition of Germany. But although, on the whole, we had no illusions as to the democratic leanings of Kühlmann and Czernin—we were only

THE RUSSIAN REVOLUTION

too well acquainted with the nature of the German and Austrian ruling classes—it must, nevertheless, be candidly admitted that we did not at the time anticipate that the *actual* proposals of the German Imperialists would be separated by such a wide gulf from the formulæ presented to us by Kühlmann on December 25th as a sort of plagiarism of the Russian Revolution. We, indeed, did not expect such an acme of impudence.

The masses of the working classes in Russia were deeply impressed by Kühlmann's reply. They read in it the fear of the ruling classes of the Central Empires in face of the discontent and growing impatience of the masses in Germany. On December 28th, a gigantic workers and soldiers' demonstration took place in Petrograd in favour of a democratic peace. But the next morning our delegates returned from Brest-Litovsk and brought those predatory demands which Kühlmann had presented on behalf of the Central Empires by way of interpretation of his so-called democratic formulæ.

At first it may appear difficult to understand what exactly were the expectations of the German diplomacy when they presented their democratic formulæ in order, two or three days later, to reveal their brutal appetites. The theoretical debates, too, about those democratic formulæ—for the most part initiated by Kühlmann himself—may seem to have been rather a risky affair. It ought to have been clear to them from the beginning that on this battlefield the diplomacy of the Central Empires could scarcely gain any laurals. But the secret of Kühlmann's conduct of diplomacy lay in that he was profoundly convinced that we would be ready to play duets with him. The trend of his thought was approximately as follows: Russia must have peace. The Bolsheviks had obtained power thanks to their fight for peace. The Bolsheviks wanted to remain in power. This was only possible on one condition, namely, the conclusion of peace. True, they had committed themselves to a definite democratic peace programme. But what were the diplomats for, if not for disguising black as white? They, the Germans, would make the position easier for the Bolsheviks by hiding their spoil and plunder beneath a democratic formula. Bolshevik diplomacy would have sufficient grounds for not desiring to probe too deeply for the political essence of their enticing formulæ, or, rather, for not revealing it to the eyes of the world. In other words, Kühlmann hoped to come to a tacit understanding with us. He would pay us back in our fine formula, and we should give him an opportunity of obtaining provinces and whole nationalities for the benefit of the Central Empires without any protest on our side. In the eyes of the German working classes, therefore, this violent annexation would receive the sanction of the Russian Revolution. When, during the negotiations, we made it clear that we were not discussing mere empty formulæ and decorative screens hiding a secret bargain, but the democratic foundations of the cohabitation of nations, Kühlmann took it as a malevolent breach of a tacit agreement. He would not for anything in the world budge even an inch from his formula of December 25th. Relying on his refined bureaucratic and legal logic, he tried his best to prove to the world that there was no difference whatever between black and white, and that it was only due to our malicious will that we were insisting on it.

Count Czernin, the representative of Austria-Hungary, played at these negotiations a part which no one would call impressive or dignified. He clumsily seconded and undertook at all critical moments, on behalf of Kühlmann, to make the most violent and cynical declarations. As against this, General Hoffman would often introduce a most refreshing note into the negotiations. Without shamming any great sympathy with the diplomatic niceties of Kühlmann, General Hoffman many times banged his soldier's boot on the table, at which the most intricate legal debates were carried on. For our part, we had not a moment's doubt that at these negotiations General Hoffman's boot was the only serious reality.

The presence of the representatives of the Kieff Rada at the negotiations was a great trump card in Kühlmann's hands. To the Ukrainian lower middle class, who were then in power, their " recognition " by the capitalist Governments of

Europe seemed the most important thing in the world. At first, the Rada had offered its services to the Allied Imperialists and got from them some pocket-money. It then sent delegates to Brest-Litovsk in order to obtain from the Austro-German Governments, behind the backs of the peoples of Russia, the recognition of their legitimate birth. Scarcely had the Kieff diplomats entered on the road of "international" relations than they manifested the same outlook and the same moral level which had hitherto been a characteristic feature of the petty Balkan politicians. Messrs. Kühlmann and Czernin, of course, did not indulge in any illusions as to the solvency of the new partner at the negotiations. But they realized quite correctly that by the attendance of the Kieff delegates the game was fated to become more complicated, but also more promising to them. At their first appearance at Brest-Litovsk the Kieff delegation defined the Ukraine as a component part of the nascent Federal Republic of Russia. That was an obvious embarrassment to the diplomats of the Central Powers, whose chief concern was to turn the Russian Republic into a new Balkan Peninsula. At their second appearance, the diplomats of the Rada declared, under the dictation of Austro-German diplomacy, that from that moment the Ukraine no longer desired to form part of the Russian Federation and would constitute henceforth an independent Republic.

In order to give the readers a clear idea of

the situation in which the Soviet Government was placed at the last stage of the peace negotiations, I think it useful to reproduce here the main passages of the speech which the author of these lines delivered, as the People's Commissioner for Foreign Affairs, at the sitting of the Central Executive Committee on February 27, 1918.

THE SPEECH OF THE PEOPLE'S COMMISSIONER FOR FOREIGN AFFAIRS.

" Comrades,—Russia of the Soviets has not only to build the new, but also to sum up the results of the past and, to a certain extent—a very large extent indeed—to settle old accounts, above all, the accounts of the present war which has now lasted three and a half years. The war has been a test of the economic resources of the belligerent nations. The fate of Russia, a poor, backward country, was, in a war of attrition, pre-determined from the beginning. In the mighty conflict of the military machines the decisive rôle belonged, in the last resort, to the ability of the respective nations to adapt their industry in the shortest possible time, and thus to turn out again and again, with constantly increasing rapidity and in ever-increasing quantities, the engines of destruction which have been wearing out in no time in this terrible slaughter of nations. At the beginning of the war every, or almost every, country, even the most backward, could be in possession of powerful engines of destruction, since those machines could be obtained from abroad. All backward countries did possess them, including Russia. But the war soon wears out its dead capital, unless it is constantly replenished. The military power of every individual country drawn into the whirlwind of the world-wide war was measured by the ability to make guns, shells, and other engines of destruction by its own means during the war itself. If the war had decided the question of the balance of power in a very short time, Russia, speaking theoretically, might have come out on the victorious side. But the war dragged on, and did so by no means accidentally. · The mere fact that during the preceding half-century all international politics had been reduced to the establishment of the so-called balance of power, that is, to the greatest possible equalization · of the military forces of the adversaries, was bound, in view of the strength and wealth of the modern capitalist nations, to make the war a protracted business. The result has been, first and foremost, the exhaustion of the poorer, less economically developed countries.

"Germany proved to be the most powerful country in the military sense, owing to the mighty development of her industry and the new, rational, up-to-date structure of that industry side by side with the archaic structure of her State. France, with her economic system largely based on small production, proved to be very much behind Germany, while even such a powerful colonial Empire as England showed herself weaker than

132

Germany, owing to the more conservative, routine-like character of her industries. When the will of History summoned revolutionary Russia to initiate peace negotiations, we had no doubt whatever that, failing the intervention of the decisive power of the world's revolutionary proletariat, we should have to pay in full for over three and a half years of war. We knew perfectly well that German Imperialism was an enemy imbued with the consciousness of its own colossal strength, as manifested so glaringly in the present war.

" All the arguments of the bourgeois cliques which keep telling us that we should have been incomparably stronger had we conducted our peace negotiations in conjunction with our Allies are fundamentally wrong. If we were to carry on, at some distant future, the peace negotiations in conjunction with the Allies, we should, in the first place, have had to go on with the war ; but seeing how our country was exhausted and weakened, its continuation, not its cessation, would have led to further exhaustion and ruin. We should thus have had to foot the bill of the war in conditions still more unfavourable to us. Even if the camp which Russia had joined on account of the international intrigues of Tsardom and the bourgeoisie —the camp, that is, at the head of which stands Great Britain—should come out of the war completely victorious (granting for the moment this rather improbable eventuality), it does not follow, comrades, that our country would also have come out victorious, since Russia, inside this victorious camp, would have been still more exhausted and ruined by the long-drawn-out war than it is now. The masters of that camp, who would have gathered all the fruits of victory—that is, England and America—would, in their treatment of our country, have displayed the same methods which were employed by Germany at the peace negotiations. It would be absurd and childish, in appraising the policy of the Imperialist countries, to start from other premises than their naked self-interest and material strength. Hence, if we, as a nation, are now weakened in the face of the Imperialist world, we are so not because we broke away from the fiery circle of the war after previously shaking off the chains of international military obligations—no, we are weakened by the same policy of Tsardom and the bourgeois classes against which we fought, as a revolutionary party, both before and during the war.

"You remember, comrades, the conditions in which our delegates went to Brest-Litovsk last time, direct from one of the sittings of the Third All-Russian Congress of Soviets. We had informed you then of the state of negotiations and of the demands of the enemy. These demands, as you no doubt remember, amounted to disguised, or rather semi-disguised, annexationist claims to Lithuania, Courland, part of Livonia, the Moon Sound Islands, and a semi-masked indemnity which we then computed at six to eight or even ten thousand million roubles. In the interval, which lasted ten days, serious disturbances broke out in Austria and strikes took place among the labouring masses there—the first act of recognition of our methods of conducting the peace negotiations on the part of the proletariat of the Central Powers in face of the annexationist demands of German Imperialism. How miserable are the allegations of the bourgeois Press, that it took us two months' talk with Kühlmann before we discovered that the German Imperialists would demand robbers' terms. No, we knew that beforehand. But we tried to turn our 'conversations' with the representatives of German Imperialism into a means of strengthening those forces which were struggling against it. We did not promise in this connection any miracles, but we asserted that our way was the only way still left at the disposal of revolutionary democracy for securing the chances of its further development.

"One may complain that the proletariat of other countries, especially of the Central Empires, is passing to an open revolutionary struggle too slowly. Yes, the *tempo* of its advance is much too slow. But in Austria-Hungary we saw a movement which assumed the proportions of a national event and which was a direct and immediate result of the Brest-Litovsk negotiations.

"Before we departed from here we discussed

the matter together, and we said that we had no reason to believe that that wave would sweep away the Austro-Hungarian militarism. Had we been convinced to the contrary, we should have certainly given the pledge so eagerly demanded from us by certain persons, namely, that we should never sign a separate treaty with Germany. I said at the time that it was impossible for us to make such a pledge, as it would have been tantamount to pledging ourselves to defeat German Imperialism. We held the secret of no such victory in our hands, and in so far as we could not pledge ourselves to change the balance and correlation of the world's powers in a very short period of time, we openly and honestly declared that the revolutionary Government might, under certain circumstances, be compelled to accept an annexationist peace. For not the acceptance of a peace forced upon us by the course of events, but an attempt to hide its predatory character from our own people would have been the beginning of the end of the revolutionary Government.

" At the same time we pointed out that we were departing for Brest in order to continue the negotiations in circumstances which were apparently becoming more favourable to us and less advantageous to our adversaries. We were watching the events in Austria-Hungary, and various circumstances made us think that, as hinted at by Socialist spokesmen in the Reichstag, Germany was on the eve of similar events.

THE RUSSIAN REVOLUTION

Such were our hopes, and then in the course of the first days of our new stay at Brest the wireless brought us via Vilna the first news that a tremendous strike movement had broken out in Berlin, which, like the movement in Austria-Hungary, was the direct result of the Brest-Litovsk negotiations. But, as it often happens, in consequence of the 'dialectical,' double-edged, character of the class struggle, it was just this powerful swing of the proletarian movement, such as Germany had never seen before, that aroused the propertied classes and caused them to close their ranks and to take up a more irreconcilable attitude. The German ruling classes are only too well imbued with the instinct of self-preservation, and they understood that any, even partial concession, under such circumstances, when they were being pressed by the masses of their own people, would have been tantamount to a capitulation before the idea of revolution. That is why, after the first period of conferences, when Kühlmann had been deliberately delaying the negotiations by either postponing the sittings or wasting them on minor questions of form, he, as soon as the strike had been suppressed and his masters, he felt, were for the time being out of danger, reverted to his old accents of complete self-confidence, and redoubled his aggressiveness. Our negotiations became complicated owing to the participation of the Kieff Rada. We reported the facts of the case last time.

THE RUSSIAN REVOLUTION

The Rada delegates made their appearance at a time when the Rada still represented a fairly strong organization in the Ukraine and when the issue of the struggle had not yet been decided. · Just at that moment we made the Rada an official offer to conclude with us a definite agreement, the principal term of which was our demand that the Rada should proclaim Kaledin and Korniloff enemies of the Revolution and refrain from interfering in our fight against them. The Kieff delegates arrived at the moment when we were cherishing hopes of coming to an agreement with it on both heads. We had already made clear to the Rada that so long as it was recognized by the Ukrainian people we should admit it to the negotiations as an independent member of the Conference. But in proportion as things in Russia and the Ukraine developed, and the antagonism between the democratic masses and the Rada was becoming deeper and deeper, the readiness of the Rada also increased to conclude any sort of peace with the Central Powers, and, if necessary, to invite German Imperialism to intervene in the internal affairs of the Ukrainian Republic in order to support the Rada against the Russian Revolution.

" On February 9th we learned that the peace negotiations between the Rada and the Central Powers had been successfully completed behind our backs. February 9th was the birthday of Prince Leopold of Bavaria, and, as is the custom in monarchical countries, the solemn, historical act of signing the treaty was fixed for this festal day—whether with the Rada's agreement or not we do not know. General Hoffman caused the artillery to fire a salute in honour of Leopold of Bavaria, having previously asked the Ukrainians' permission to do so, as, according to that treaty, Brest-Litovsk had been incorporated with the Ukraine.

" However, at the very moment when General Hoffman was asking the Kieff Rada for permission to fire a salute in honour of Prince Leopold, events had advanced so far that, with the exception of Brest-Litovsk, but little territory was left under the Rada's authority. On the strength of telegrams which we had received from Petrograd we officially informed the delegates of the Central Powers that the Kieff Rada was no longer in existence—a fact which was by no means immaterial for the course of the peace negotiations. We proposed to Count Czernin to send representatives, accompanied by our officers, to the territory of the Ukraine in order to see on the spot whether his co-partner, the Kieff Rada, was still in existence or not. Czernin at first seemed to jump at the idea, but when we raised the question whether the treaty with the Kieff delegation would only be signed after the return of his messengers or not, he began to hesitate and promised to consult Kühlmann, and having done so, sent us a reply in the negative. This was on February 8th, and on the following day they were obliged to sign the treaty. That brooked no delay, not only because of Prince Leopold's birthday, but also because of a more serious circumstance, which, of course, Kühlmann had explained to Czernin: 'If we send our representatives to the Ukraine now, they may find that the Rada is no longer in existence, and then we should have to face the Russian delegates only, which of course would greatly thwart our chances at the negotiations.' We were told by the Austro-Hungarian delegates: 'Leave alone the question of principles, place the problem on a practical footing—then the German delegates will try to meet you. It is impossible that the Germans should desire to continue the war for the sake, for instance, of the Moon Sound Islands, if you formulate your demands more concretely. . . .' We answered: 'Very well, we are ready to test the conciliatory attitude of your colleagues, the German delegates. So far we have been discussing the question of the right of self-determination of Lithuanians, Poles, Letts, Esthonians, etc., and have elucidated the fact that there is no chance for the self-determination of these small nations. Let us now see what kind of self-determination you intend to allot to the Russian people, and what are the military strategical plans and devices behind your seizure of the Moon Islands. The Moon Islands, as part of the Esthonian Republic, as a possession of the Russian Federal Republic, have a defensive value, while in the hands of Germany they are means of offence and constitute a menace to the most vital centres of our country, particularly to Petrograd.' But, of course, Hoffman had not the slightest intention of making any concessions. Then the decisive moment came. We could not declare war—we were too weak. The army was in a state of complete internal dissolution. In order to save our country from ruin it was necessary to re-establish the internal organization of the labouring masses. This moral union could be established only by constructive work in the villages, in the workshop and the factory. The masses, who had passed through the colossal suffering and the catastrophic experiences of the war, had to be brought back to the fields and factories, where they could be rejuvenated morally and physically by work and thus be enabled to create the necessary internal discipline. There was no other way of salvation for our country, which had to pay the penalty for the sins committed by Tsardom and the bourgeoisie. We were forced to get out of the war and lead our army out of the slaughter. At the same time we declared to German Imperialism, straight in the face: ' The peace terms which you force us to accept are those of violence and plunder. We cannot allow you, diplomats, to tell the German workers : ' You branded our demands as annexationist;; look here, those demands have been signed by the Russian Revolution !' Yes, we are weak, we cannot fight at present, but we have enough of revolutionary courage to tell you that we will never of our own free will sign the terms which you are writing with your sword across the bodies of the living peoples.' We refused to give our signatures, and I believe, comrades, that we acted as we ought to have acted.

" Comrades, I do not want to say that a further advance of the Germans against us is out of the question. Such a statement would be too risky, considering the power of the German Imperialist Party. But I think that by the position we have taken up on the question we have made any advance a very embarrassing affair for the German militarists. What would happen if they should nevertheless advance? There is only one answer to this question. If it is still possible to raise the spirit in the most revolutionary and healthy elements in our exhausted country, reduced as it is to desperate straits, if it is still possible for Russia to rise for the defence of our Revolution and the territories of the Revolution, it is possible only as a result of the present situation, as a result of our coming out of the war and of our refusal to sign the peace treaty."

THE SECOND WAR AND THE SIGNING OF PEACE.

The German Government, during the first days after the breaking off of the negotiations, hesitated, uncertain as to which course to choose. The politicians and diplomats thought apparently, that the chief thing had been accomplished, and that there was no need to run after our signatures. The military, however, were in all circumstances prepared to break through the framework outlined by the German Government in the Brest-Litovsk treaty. Professor Kriege, adviser to the German delegation, told one of our delegates that in the present conditions there could be no question of a new German offensive against Russia. Count Mirbach, then at the head of the German mission in Russia, left for Berlin assuring us that a satisfactory agreement on the exchange of prisoners had been reached. But all this did not prevent General Hoffman from announcing, on the fifth day after the breaking off of the negotiations, the end of the armistice, the seven days' notice being antedated by him from the day of the last sitting at Brest. It would be truly out of place to waste time here in righteous indignation at this dishonourable act, for it is but in keeping with the general diplomatic and military morality of all the governing classes.

The new German offensive developed under conditions which were deadly to Russia. Instead of the agreed seven days' warning, we only had two days'. This spread a panic in the ranks of the army, already in a state of chronic dissolution. There could scarcely be any question of resistance. The soldiers would not believe that the Germans would advance, after we had declared the state of war at an end. The panic-stricken retreat paralysed even the will of those individual regiments which were ready to take up fighting positions. In the working-class quarters of Petrograd and Moscow the indignation at the treacherous and truly buccaneering German attack knew no bounds. The workers were ready, in those tragic days and nights, to enlist in the army in their tens of thousands. But the necessary organization was lagging far behind. Individual guerrilla detachments, full of enthusiasm, perceived their helplessness at the first serious encounter with the German regular troops, and this was, of course, followed by a further depression of spirits. The old army, long ago mortally wounded, was falling to pieces, and was only blocking up all ways and by-ways. The new army, on the other hand, was arising much too slowly amidst the general exhaustion and the terrible dislocation of industry and transport. The only real serious obstacle in the path of the German advance was the huge distances. . . .

Austria-Hungary had her eyes chiefly on the Ukraine. Through its delegates the Rada had made a direct request to the Central Empires for military help against the Soviets, which by that time had obtained complete victory throughout Ukrainia. In this way the Ukrainian lower middle-class democracy, in its fight with the workers and the poorest peasantry, had voluntarily opened the gates to foreign invasion.

At the same time the Government of Svinhufvud was seeking the help of German bayonets against the Finnish proletariat. German militarism was assuming quite openly, in the face of the whole world, the rôle of executioner of the Russian workers and peasants' revolution.

In the ranks of our party there arose a heated discussion as to whether we should, under such conditions, submit to the German ultimatum and sign a new treaty which—we were all quite convinced of that—would contain far more onerous conditions than those we had been offered at Brest-Litovsk. The representatives of one school of thought considered that at the present moment, when the Germans were effectively intervening in the internal struggles on the territory of the Russian Republic, it was unthinkable to make peace in one part of Russia and remain passive whilst in the north and south the German troops were establishing a regime of bourgeois dictatorship. Another school of thought, at the head of which stood Lenin, argued that every interval, every breathing space, however short, would be of the greatest value for the internal consolidation of Russia and for the restoration of her capacity for self-defence. After our absolute inability to defend ourselves at the present moment from the attacks of the enemy had been demonstrated so tragically before the whole country and the whole world, our conclusion of peace would be understood everywhere as an act forced on us by the cruel law of the correlation of forces. It would be mere childishness to base our action on abstract revolutionary morals. The question at issue was not how to perish with honour, but how, in the end, we could live through to victory. The Russian revolution wants to live, must live, and must by all possible means refuse to be drawn into battle far beyond her strength : she must win time in the expectation that the revolutionary movement in the West would come to her aid. German Imperialism was still at close and fierce grip with British and American militarism. Only for this reason was it possible to conclude peace between Germany and Russia. We must not let this opportunity slip by. The well-being of the Revolution was the supreme law ! We must accept the peace which we dared not refuse ; we must gain some time for intensive work in the interior, including the reconstruction of our army.

At the Congress of the Communist Party, just as at the fourth Congress of the Soviets, those in favour of peace were in a majority. Many of those who in January had been opposed to signing the Brest peace treaty were now in favour of peace. " At that time," said they, " our signature would have been understood by the British and French workers as a miserable capitulation without any attempt to avoid it; even the base insinuations of the Anglo-French chauvinists about a secret agreement between the Soviet Government and the Germans might have met with some acceptance in certain sections of the Western European workers, had we then signed the peace treaty. But after our refusal to sign, after the new German offensive against us, after our attempt at resistance, after our military weakness has been demonstrated to the whole world with such awful clearness, no one will dare reproach us with having capitulated without a struggle." The Brest-Litovsk treaty, the second, more onerous edition, was duly signed and ratified.

In the meantime, in the Ukraine and in Finland the executioners were going on with their grim work, threatening more and more the most vital centres of Great Russia. Thus, the question of the very existence of Russia as an independent country became indissolubly bound up with the question of a European revolution.

CONCLUSION.

When our party was assuming the reins of Government, we knew beforehand what difficulties we should undoubtedly meet on our way. Economically the country had been exhausted by the war to the last degree. The Revolution had destroyed the old administrative machinery without having had the opportunity of creating a new one in its place. Millions of workers had been forcibly torn away from the economic life of the country, thrown out of their class, and morally and mentally shattered by three years of war. A colossal war industry on an insufficiently developed economic foundation had sucked up the very life-blood of the nation, and its demobilization presented the greatest difficulties. The phenomena inseparable from economic and political anarchy had spread widely throughout the country. The Russian peasantry had been for centuries welded together by the barbarous discipline of the land and bent down from above by the iron discipline of Tsardom. The state of our economic development had undermined the one discipline and the Revolution destroyed the other. Psychologically, the Revolution meant an awakening of human individuality in the peasant masses. The anarchical form in which this awakening found expression was but the inevitable result of the previous repression. It will only be possible to arrive at the establishment of a new order of things, based on the control of production by the producers themselves, by a general internal deliverance from the anarchical forms of the Revolution.

On the other hand, the propertied classes, although forcibly removed from power, refuse to give up their positions without a fight. The Revolution has raised in an acute form the question of private property in land and the means of production, that is, the question of the life and death of the exploiting classes. Politically this means a constant—sometimes covert, sometimes overt—bitter civil war. In its turn, civil war necessarily brings in its train anarchist tendencies in the movement of the labouring masses.

In view of the dislocation of finance, industry,

transport, and the food supply, a protracted civil war, therefore, is bound to cause gigantic difficulties in the way of the constructive work of organization. Nevertheless, the Soviet regime has every right to look forward to the future with confidence. Only an exact inventory of the resources of the country.; only a national universal plan of organization of production.; only a prudent and economical distribution of all products can save the country. And this is just Socialism. Either a descent to the state of a mere colony, or a Socialist transformation—such is the alternative which faces our country.

This war has undermined the foundations of the entire capitalist world, and in this lies our invincible strength. The Imperialist ring which is choking us will be broken by a proletarian revolution. We no more doubt this for one moment than we ever doubted the final downfall of Tsardom during the long decades of our underground work.

To struggle, to close our ranks, to establish discipline of labour and a Socialist order, to increase the productivity of labour, and not to be balked by any obstacle—such is our watchword. History is working for us. A proletarian revolution in Europe and America will break out sooner or later, and it will free not only the Ukraine, Poland, Lithuania, Courland, and Finland, but the whole of suffering humanity.

Printed in Great Britain by

OXFORD, BRINDLEY, LIMITED

WOKING AND LONDON

ar and Revolution in Asiatic Russia   By M. PHILIPS PRICE

Demy 8vo.   8s. 6d. net.

"One of the best books of travel that have appeared for many years."
Everyman.

Russia and the Struggle for Peace   By MICHAEL FARBMAN

rown 8vo.   5s. net.

"I would make Michael S. Farbmau's 'Russia and the Struggle for eace' compulsory in all schools. This is a book to sweep the cobwebs way for ever. We here learn the actual truth for the first time about he Revolution."—*Evening News.*

"A singularly valuable addition to our knowledge. Nowhere could ne find a clearer or more obviously truthful account of the great pheaval."—*The Herald.*

hree Aspects of the Russian Revolution   By EMILE VANDERVELDE

Translated by JEAN E. H. FINDLAY

rown 8vo.   5s. net.   Postage 5d.

"A valuable and original series of notes on revolutionary Russia."— *aily News.*

From Autocracy to Bolshevism

emy 8vo.   By Baron GRAVENITZ   5s. net.

"A deeply interesting book."—*Edinburgh Evening News.*

The Spirit of Russia

Studies in History, Literature, and Philosophy

By THOMAS GARRIGUE MASARYK

Sometime Professor of Philosophy at the Czech University of Prague ; Lecturer
at the School for Slavonic Studies at London University, King's College

TRANSLATED FROM THE GERMAN BY EDEN AND CEDAR PAUL

Demy 8vo.　　　　*2 vols. of about 500 pages each.*　　　　*32s. net.*

The author is widely known on the Continent for his championship (on
"realist" lines) of the cause of small nationalities, and in particular for
his courageous defence of the claims of his native Bohemia. His writing
on philosophical and sociological topics, some in Czech and others in
German, have secured for him a well-established position in the field of
abstract thought.   From youth onwards he has been interested in Russia
and the work now announced is the fruit of many years' study of Russian
literature and of prolonged and direct personal acquaintance with the
Russian people. The book will serve, not merely to explain to Western
Europe the Russia that made the revolution, but to guide us in our
interpretation of the post-revolutionary developments.

The Romance of the Romanoffs   By JOSEPH McCABE

Author of "The Tyranny of Shams," "The Soul of Europe," etc.

Demy 8vo.　　　　ILLUSTRATED.　　　　*10s. 6d. net.*

" The dynasty flaunts its brutal, sordid, attractive and romantic career
through his pages."—*The Times.*
" He has produced a picture which is complete and admirably clear."—
Glasgow Herald.

Japan at the Cross Roads

By A. M. POOLEY

Editor of "The Secret Memoirs of Count Hayashi," etc., etc.

Demy 8vo.　　　　*10s. 6d. net. Postage 6a.*

" Extremely critical and of exceptional interest."—*Daily News.*
"Is arrestingly candid and absorbingly interesting."—*Glasgow Herald.*

LONDON : GEORGE ALLEN & UNWIN LIMITED

CPSIA information can be obtained
at www.ICGtesting.com
Printed in the USA
BVOW11s1129040817

491172BV00020B/382/P

9 781333 737054